Sun Tzu's *The Art of War* for the Modern Lawyer

Giles translation

Daniel J. Rothman

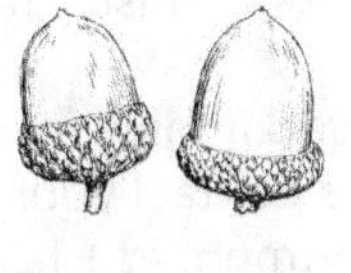

Hog Press

Hog Press
an imprint of Culicidae Press
PO Box 5069
Madison, WI 53705-5069
USA
culicidaepress.com
editor@culicidaepress.com

ISBN: 978-1-941892-84-8

Library of Congress Control Number: 2024937026

Cover design and interior layout © 2024 by polytekton

twitter.com/culicidaepress – facebook.com/culicidaepress
threads.net/culicidaepress – instagram.com/culicidaepress

Our books may be purchased in bulk for promotional, educational, and/or business use. Please contact your local bookseller or the Culicidae Press Sales Department at +1-515-462-0278 or by email at sales@culicidaepress.com

Table of Contents

Introduction   4

I. Laying Plans   6
II. Waging War   23
III. Attack by Stratagem   33
IV. Tactical Dispositions   45
V. Energy   56
VI. Weak Points and Strong   68
VII. Maneuvering   86
VIII. Variation in Tactics   102
IX. The Army on the March   112
X. Terrain   128
XI. The Nine Situations   142
XII. The Attack by Fire   163
XIII. The Use of Spies   170

About the Author   179

Introduction

Lawyers are the swords of this century. Words are weapons now.
John Dutton, in conversation with his son Jamie Dutton,
future lawyer, *Yellowstone* TV series, Season 2.

The fact that a text, from so long ago, still carries so much weight not only in its intended area of warfare but also in business and law, as well as many other areas, is a testament to the awareness of human nature and wisdom of Sun Tzu himself. There is a 'best way' to go when facing a decision on the way forward in many areas of human effort. At the top level of auto racing for example, you often find twenty of the best race car drivers in the world at a particular track during a race weekend. They each will take practice laps and explore the track but as you can see from watching qualifying and the race itself, all will agree with very little variance the best way around that track. Although tracks change from racing course to racing course, a driver will study every scenario and look for the 'best way'.

The best way is also present in each legal case that a lawyer takes on. The purpose of this book is to give you the tools that you need, to look for the best way in any legal case that you find yourself dealing with. In racing and in law there is only the win. Even when you know the fastest way, there can be other issues that make you tap the brakes too soon going into a turn or hit the gas too late coming out of a corner. Human error or unanticipated testimony can affect your performance, just like weather and chance can affect the racing driver's performance. What we must do is look for the best possible racing line and prepare as best as we can on each case to run it the 'best way' available.

It must be a constant endeavor to analyze the factors presented here. Minamoto Musashi said, "mastering swordsmanship takes one thousand days to learn and ten thousand days to refine."[1] Law school takes approximately one thousand days, including the BAR exam, yet the process of refining your skills to their utmost is ongoing from the first day of your legal career to the last.

---

[1] Miyamoto Musashi, *The Book of the Five Rings.*

I. Laying Plans

1. Sun Tzu said: The art of war is of vital importance to the State.

The art of litigation is the culmination of all that a lawyer does for their Client/State. It is of vital importance, as required by rules of ethics and our moral obligation to our clients, to put forward their case in the best possible light, as well as we are able to.

2. It is a matter of life and death, a road either to safety or to ruin. Hence it is a subject of inquiry which can on no account be neglected.

Our profession is one which involves winning and losing. In many cases it involves absolute success or destruction for a client. They can lose their company or fortune in a lawsuit or be imprisoned for life. Unlike other professions or sports, you can lose and live to fight another day. In law, our clients often face a fate as significant to them as life or death. Do the facts and law carry the day or is it the presentation of the facts and the law that determines the outcome?

3. The art of war, then, is governed by five constant factors, to be taken into account in one's deliberations, when seeking to determine the conditions obtaining in the field.

4. These are: (1) The Moral Law; (2) Heaven; (3) Earth; (4) The Commander; (5) Method and discipline.

Each of these factors relate to what you must do to prepare and how to proceed with courtroom conflict.

5, 6. The Moral Law causes the people to be in complete accord with their ruler, so that they will follow him regardless of their lives, undismayed by any danger.

Clients know they may survive or not, based on the outcome of our case with them. In any case, they will come to you and ask how you recommend they proceed. They will want to think that you truly believe what you say is accurate and is the best path forward. In other instances, they will hear your opinion and question your judgment. You will know it is the best way forward, but you will need to make the client, who is not well versed in law, understand why you are correct. Keep in mind any kind of *guaranteed* statement is unethical in many jurisdictions. You must impress upon the client that although no lawyer can or should try to guarantee a particular outcome, what you propose has the best available chance of success.

7. Heaven signifies night and day, cold and heat, times and seasons.

There can always be variables in conditions, be it a jury trial in a rural courthouse without proper air conditioning on a hot day, a visual or audible distraction of nearby construction outside of the courtroom window or other factors that may distract your jury. Additionally, the strain of weather may affect your team in more complex litigation matters. Many jurors have been put off by the thought of coming to the courthouse during snow-filled winter months. They may gaze out the windows during key moments to look at the weather, and they must be redirected. Weather can have a significant effect on the stamina of either the jury or your team. Weather can also be any feature of local origin that has an impact on people. Anything can be distracting to your team or the jury. One person may hate a snowstorm as it makes it hard to get around while another may look at a snowstorm and feel they are missing out on fresh powder for skiing. Another example is upcoming holidays. Christmas or other holidays can often cause stress and can be a distraction. Never underestimate how the jury may be distracted by any of a number of things that are going on in their world you may not even know of. Frequent highlighting of key moments or facts of the case are always important and showing sympathy to the jury's 'plight', such as in jury selection, is always worth a few moments of your time.

8. Earth comprises distances, great and small; danger and security; open ground and narrow passes; the chances of life and death.

Even in the courtroom, terrain is key. In a criminal case for example, does the prosecutor want to sit closer to the jury so that when their witness is on direct, they have more of a natural instinct of directing their statements to the jury, i.e., make more eye contact because they are already looking toward the jury? Or does the prosecutor want the defendant sitting nearer to the jury so that when he talks to his attorney, he says something incriminating, that they may hear, which would not have been admissible, or maybe they will just seem to get mad at their attorney, causing the jury to believe that perhaps it is correct that this defendant could have lost their temper, as the victim stated what had occurred on the offence date. You should always be willing to do anything that can increase your chances of victory.

9. The Commander stands for the virtues of wisdom, sincerity, benevolence, courage, and strictness.

If you lose your credibility by a bad impeachment or misstatement during trial, then you will lose everything with the jury. Often the jury does not understand the case material or law and makes their choices based on who they like or who they trust. You must also be firm, but not too harsh, as you risk losing the jury if they grow to dislike you. If they do not like you, they will consciously or unconsciously look for reasons to vote against you. Regardless of the accuracy of your arguments or statements, if you offend them in some way, you are giving your opposition a substantial advantage.

10. By method and discipline are to be understood the marshaling of the army in its proper subdivisions, the graduations of rank among the officers, the maintenance of roads by which supplies may reach the army, and the control of military expenditure.

You are the general and the client is the 'state' or 'sovereign' that you are beholden to. Although there may be certain obligations to the client, the attorney is in full command of the army. There can be assistants and law clerks and second-chair attorneys but they all must know their proper roles and only be given duties which they can handle well. In significant cases you will not be able to handle every detail on your own. It is important to have a system which is in place to allow clear lines of supply and communication between you and your staff. Each member in your team must be organizing their material in a uniform way for ease of use by other members of the team. Trial notebooks must be put together uniformly so that an assistant may supply you with the right document for an impeachment or other key question during a cross, or sidebar argument in front of the judge requiring just the right case law. If this is not done, the flow can be lost in front of a jury or a key evidentiary argument can be lost. It is also important to make sure even in a modern liberal office that a structure can be in place so that certain staff always take direction from higher-ranking staff without question. The last thing that you would want to do during precious trial prepetition time is to have meetings with certain team members to deal with ego-related issues. Also, in the modern courtroom it is a requirement for your information to flow down key 'roads' to the battlefield, so that your technology is compatible with what is present in the courtroom. You should ask the judge or clerk for permission to do a test run to make sure your tech is compatible and ready for use. Also, you must consider every member of the team's ability and familiarity with technology if you plan to use it to communicate with your team or have other members use your tech to present videos or other visual aides to the jury.

11. These five matters should be familiar to every general: he who knows them will be victorious; he who knows them not will fail.

Every case has particular facts and governing law for that specific case; however there are universal strategic aspects that must be analyzed as well.

12. Therefore, in your deliberations, when seeking to determine the military conditions, let them be made the basis of a comparison.

You can't very well tell the client your thoughts on the wisdom of going to trial vs taking a deal, etc. without first being aware of how the battle would play out in court. You must be able to explain to the client how the trial may go and what may make it shift in directions and what issues the outcome will turn on.

13. (1) Which of the two sovereigns is imbued with the Moral law? (2) Which of the two generals has most ability? (3) With whom lie the advantages derived from Heaven and Earth?

(4) On which side is discipline most rigorously enforced? (5) Which army is stronger? (6) On which side are officers and men more highly trained? (7) In which army is there the greater constancy both in reward and punishment?

1. Moral law or who is 'right' or 'just' is key to any trial. A prosecutor will claim moral high ground in protection of the community. A criminal defense lawyer will claim to be saving the innocent from being convicted for a crime they did not commit. A plaintiff's lawyer will claim to present the wronged citizen seeking their just due under our laws. A civil defense lawyer will contend that the plaintiff seeks what they do not deserve and that they seek to undermine our system. Any lawyer may have the 'right position' in court *but* they must convince the jury not only that they are correct, but they must make the jury want to rule in your favor. They need to believe you *should* win, so they feel they are on the side of right and can live with whatever their final decision is.

2. Of course, the skill of the lawyer will play a large part in the outcome in a trial just as in war, but other factors may overcome the skill of the lawyer.

3. Each side will have laws and facts that are in their favor. By the time trial occurs, it is too late to adjust the terrain, so pre-trial actions must be done with the future trial landscape in mind. A sympathetic victim in a criminal or tort case will be an advantage. A super-rich criminal or civil defendant, if known to the jury, will be a natural hindrance.

4. Discipline of the lawyer is key. Often times, when a lawyer loses their cool, they communicate to a jury that a fact or piece of testimony is hurting their case. It is important to not let the jury see when something hurts. Do not underestimate that a juror often does not understand completely what is going on and it may be your demeanor that brings them back to the attention of a painful aspect of the case. Discipline of witnesses is key here as well. Although there are rules regarding coaching a witness, everything within the rules must be done to prepare them with

mock cross examinations and practicing direct run-throughs. Of course, conversely, should the opportunity arise, it can be very productive to get the opposition lawyer or witness to lose their cool.

5. Strength of one side vs the other is a key factor to understand. Often times one side is far stronger than the other in terms of resources or other advantages. A court-appointed lawyer taking on the state in a criminal case is an obvious example. Such factors are hard to manipulate but should be considered when deciding if trial or a deal is worthy. In trial it is often fair game to point out the unfair strength of the other side. For example, in a criminal case the defense can note the size and resources of the state, such as the number of detectives they have when noting a lead was not followed up on that could have given evidence favorable for the defendant.

6. On which side are officers and men more highly trained? This is another factor not under a lawyer's control. The state in a criminal case may have an officer witness who has testified a hundred times, or in a civil case a professional expert may have testified in similar cases often as well. Again, that can be used against them in questioning. A psychologist who has found a person to be sane in dozens of trials vs none to be insane; an alcohol expert who disregards studies regarding flaws in testing, etc. Just because a witness may sound like a good expert does not discount their prejudices. A detective with years of experience may be afraid their credibility will be destroyed for the rest of their career if they admit to a mistake in a particular case. An expert who worked for the state for years and found in their favor most of the time who goes into the private sector and then amazingly changes their opinions to predominantly defense-friendly. The history of witness findings must be explored in depositions or pre-trial investigation. Conversely, there is value in experience when looking for your own expert. It may cost more, but if you have a great expert, it can be worth every penny.

7. In which army is there the greater constancy both in reward and punishment? Again, motivations of witnesses are key; from experts who work for money to eyewitnesses who may have prejudices to one side or the other. Could a win in a big case lead to an officer getting a promotion? What is an expert witness being paid per trial or per hour? Certainly, a win for an expert in one case may lead to more lucrative cases in the future and a loss the opposite. Also, if an officer involved in a losing case is seen as responsible then the loss could affect that officer's chances for promotions, raises, and a larger retirement. It can be said that a detective may have thousands of dollars over their lifetime on the line when they are testifying.

14. **By means of these seven considerations I can forecast victory or defeat.**

These considerations must be taken into account when looking at every case and picking your strategy or when advising a client of their chances at trial.

15. **The general that hearkens to my counsel and acts upon it, will conquer: let such a one be retained in command! The general that hearkens not to my counsel nor acts upon it, will suffer defeat – let such a one be dismissed!**

You may be limited in your case by time or money for experts, etc. but you can't afford to not properly analyze a case before deciding to and/or going to trial.

16. **While heading the profit of my counsel, avail yourself also of any helpful circumstances over and beyond the ordinary rules.**

Of all the rules that govern the practice of law the one that I often feel is the most important is to zealously represent your client's interests. All paths forward can only be accurately seen and judged in the light offered by this rule. Every lawyer is governed by ethics rules as well, and they must be, but you must strive to find any shred of material that can help you and your client on your path to victory. You can't follow the same plan in every case like a robot. Each case will yield a special source or opportunity for an advantage that is unique to that case.

17. According as circumstances are favorable, one should modify one's plans.

Some lawyers may grow too relaxed when handling the same type of case over and over again cases like a Drunk driving DUI case. Although fighting a battle on the same battlefield may offer some clarity or appropriate repetition, the number of variables or unique aspects of a case need to be given their necessary attention. Of course, you need to plan your attack points based on what you can see as the stronger aspects of your case and the weaker points of your opponent's case. If you think a particular prosecutor is set for trial on a bigger matter when you are set to go to trial, then press that advantage as they may be more likely to deal, or if they go to trial, their attention will be divided.

18. All warfare is based on deception.

The lawyer is obligated as part of our legal system to provide knowledge of what they intend to argue or at least what evidence they plan to present per their local discovery rules. Discovery can even be required by a criminal defendant if they trigger obligations regarding reciprocal discovery. However, Sun Tzu's deception principle is still key to the practice of law. It relates to actions in discovery regarding sending to the other side a key document but supplying it in the midst of an entire box of several hundred documents that are not dangerous to your plan of attack. Never forget the nature of our system is "adversarial".

This pillar of Sun Tzu's concepts requires that a lawyer play out their arguments and attacks in such a way as to not forecast their actions whenever possible. You can spend months and years on a case and still have surprises to deal with and to deliver. You may sit on a timing issue with an alleged victim or other detail that goes unnoticed all the way until trial. Do not presume that the opposition knows where you are going, and be subtle about it. For example, if you are going to point out to a witness on cross that a calibration log required by state law was not completed in a timely fashion, set the witness up with questions that go to the importance of it *before* showing them the document and then asking after you have pointed out the flaw, what the importance is. Ask the witness who was supposed to have calibrated a machine for alcohol breath testing about the local rules requiring the testing and their agency's policies for doing it, as they must agree with you, or better still get impeachment documents prepared to lock them in. Most jurisdictions don't require disclosure of a document presented only for impeachment purposes.

It is also important to be familiar with your jurisdiction's requirements on ethics and fair play. It is not enough to do or not do something based on your impression of what is fair. To provide something in discovery that is not required to be disclosed is a hindrance to your client. You must be familiar with your jurisdiction's rules so that you do not violate them, but you also must do everything within the bounds of the rules to increase your client's chance of success or you are not truly serving them professionally. The case must be as important to you as it is to them.

One of the most challenging aspects of litigation is disclosing enough evidence or strategy to get an opponent to see the strength of your case and be willing to offer a good resolution while at the same time not tipping off your opponent to material or issues, they can take time and prepare to successfully counter. Choosing what strategic planning to disclose to use as leverage and what to hold in reserve, if the matter goes to trial, is arguably the single most challenging issue to resolve in each case.

19. Hence, when able to attack, we must seem unable; when using our forces, we must seem inactive; when we are near, we must make the enemy believe we are far away; when far away, we must make him believe we are near.

Many people expect lawyers to be bombastic and full of themselves in their daily manner and how they carry themselves. The best lawyers often hide their abilities when they can. Often, criminal defense lawyers will threaten prosecutors with crushing victory or ethics claims, etc. This just makes the prosecutor more engaged and more willing to focus their limited time on your case and not others from their caseload. Great lawyers, when meeting for a pre-trial conference or other more benign courthouse activity, will often embrace cordial approaches to opposing lawyers, such as engaging them with jokes or funny stories, compliments, or other niceties. There is much to gain from kindness when you can and much to lose from anger or worthless antagonizing. Sometimes you want the opponent to know how many chips you have so they know you can out-bet them, and sometimes you should want to keep your chips in a pile and not stacked, so they don't know how many you have. There can be a time and place to show your opponent your strength, but it should not be displayed too early or in such a way that motivates your opponent to prepare harder.

20. Hold out baits to entice the enemy. Feign disorder and crush him.

Many talented courtroom maestros may seem disheveled or aloof when not in front of a judge or jury. Especially with a new opponent, there is no reason to show how talented you may be up front. There is no reason to tell another lawyer how hard you may be working or how you think depositions will show certain holes in the other side's case. At some point you will tip your hand to a degree as needed to garner a plea offer, etc., but never do so anymore then you must until you are ready to deliver a crushing blow to the opponent's case.

Complaining about how many cases you have in passing to the other side may make them, even subconsciously, not fear you as they should or not believe that you will put as much time as you should into the case. Of course, you don't want to make a prosecutor think that you have so many cases that you are bragging about income, but perhaps even noting family issues like your kid's after-school activities making it so you have to take them all over, etc. are taxing you. If you left a prosecutor's office, for example, and are now working as a defense lawyer, then you should complain about aspects that frustrate you that they don't have to deal with. You can note a nagging client in another case or office management issues like monthly billing headaches, rising cost of overhead, etc.

In each of your cases, you will need to decide early on if you want to project great strength at the risk of gaining more effort from your opponent or be seeming disorganized or at odds early on, so your opponent doesn't feel a need to focus their effort on your case.

21. If he is secure at all points, be prepared for him. If he is in superior strength, evade him.

For lawyers this can include delaying the matter. You should not be going forward on a motion to suppress or trial, etc. if you think more time *may* benefit your case. Things can happen, witnesses move, victims change their mind about what should happen to a defendant or wanting to have to testify, etc. If you have dodged a weak point as long as you can and you must engage, then you must prepare as best as you can in the hopes that time (and your other tactics) have weakened the opponent's position. If your opponent is in a position that you know you can't beat him in at all, then there is nothing to lose by waiting. If their position becomes stronger, then it doesn't matter as they already had an insurmountable position, but time has the power to erode the strongest of mountains.

22. If your opponent is of choleric temper, seek to irritate him. Pretend to be weak, that he may grow arrogant.

If backed into a corner in trial, provocation of the other lawyer or a witness may turn things in your favor or cause the opposition to stumble. As long as you do not irritate the jury, then objections or other annoying swipes directed at the opposing attorney may be beneficial. Everyone, when irritated, can lose sight of a key issue, or forget a key point. Even if they don't miss it, irritation can alter the effectiveness of their delivery of a pocket of questions that are critical to the case. If it does not affect your standing with the jury, then it is worth a shot. The same can be said for witnesses. For example, pointing out that an expert is not a doctor by accidentally calling him doctor and then correcting yourself may annoy the witness or make them too eager to get back at you in some way.

Although irritating an opponent can be helpful, it is unwise to motivate them to work harder at a time in the process when they can still prepare. Annoying the opponent at trial is beneficial as they have already done most of what they need to prepare. Before trial you don't want an opponent, like a prosecutor, spending their limited time focusing on your case. Also, provocation should not be centered around telling the opponent you will win or how strong your case may be. There will be times when you have to point out favorable points to secure a better offer, but bragging is never the way. Often times you may want to try to seem slightly unsteady or not ready before trial, especially after plea talks have faltered. You want an opponent, especially one who has great advantages, to feel that they need not worry about the outcome of key issues.

23. If he is taking his ease, give him no rest. If his forces are united, separate them.

The workload of your opponent is key, especially in criminal cases. Prosecutors and public defenders often have many more cases than they would like to or think they have the time for. Being able to dive deep into one case is an option left mostly for private-pay lawyers. Although the state and plaintiff have the burden, they should be sure to list any possible witness they can. Even if a prosecutor or plaintiff thinks there is only a remote chance they will be needed, it is best to list them just in case, and that leaves more witnesses for the other side to ponder, of course.

If your jurisdiction allows, review the trial calendar. See what the other side has for upcoming trials and keep them busy at times when you know they may not be able to dedicate as much focus and prep as they may want. Divide the time they have to build their cases that are tantamount to their forces. Wait for the right time to file a motion to suppress when their calendar is already looking full, for example.

24. **Attack him where he is unprepared, appear where you are not expected.**

This is of great importance to the lawyer's cause. Depositions and other steps are to be taken to find flaws in the opponent's case without broadcasting what they are. Also, during the deposition or investigation a subtle approach needs to be made so that the witness doesn't see the flaw until they are committed to an under-oath statement or filed report that lets you prove your point. Although a rock-solid impeachment moment can be saved for trial with no worries, it is always best to try to keep these subtle and in your pocket until the day of trial so that the witness or lawyer can't prepare and make adjustments. Of course, doing so while asking the questions to lock them in can be difficult. While at trial, you may be sure to cover key material and the end and beginning of a direct or cross; in a deposition you will want to casually try to bring it up in the middle. Never put your strong deposition points in the beginning. Let the witness get tired or bored with hours of insubstantial material and then bring up the best material after they are fatigued in some way.

Another good option is that, if you want to lock a witness into a lie or impeachment that they can't wiggle out of and you want your opponent to see ahead of trial, the weakness that comes from the inconsistency or other issue, do it at their deposition. It may be wise to, in essence, impeach them at the deposition and get them locked in so, if it is strong enough it is locked in still for trial if needed but shows the state a flaw that may motivate a better offer. Of course, you have to be very careful in evaluating whether the impeachment will stand if trial comes or if you have given your opponent a great chance to correct the error ahead of time.

25. These military devices, leading to victory, must not be divulged beforehand.

As Denzel Washington says in *Training Day*, "This is chess, not checkers." [2] All of the above is essential to winning and therefore you have to achieve the goals and take the advantages noted by Sun Tzu without highlighting the points until trial, *if* at all possible. However, the vast majority of cases end without trial, which of course requires that you get your opponent to see that they don't have a good chance to 'win'. You have to do that without letting them know exactly what you plan to do if you have to fight it out. This is an extremely delicate balance that varies from case to case, but of course it is a pivotal consideration that needs to be thoroughly analyzed. You may want to disclose your overall strategy so they see your strength and the wisdom of taking an offer, without disclosing your exact tactics so they can't prepare to counter the specific approach you will take.

26. Now the general who wins a battle makes many calculations in his temple where the battle is fought. The general who loses a battle makes but few calculations beforehand. Thus, do many calculations lead to victory, and

---

[2] Training Day, 2001, https://www.imdb.com/title/tt0139654/ accessed on 22 July 2023.

few calculations to defeat: how much more no calculation at all! It is by attention to this point that I can foresee who is likely to win or lose.

You bill by the hour, more than likely. For monetary reason as well as for zealous representation, a realistic analysis of your case must be done ahead of time so you know what you will need to take the case. You must try to contemplate as many possibilities as you can, whether remote or likely. Many lawyers are subject to permission to withdraw from a case from the court. The Court may order a lawyer to finish a case even if they are no longer getting paid, especially the closer you are to trial. You will need to find out all you can about the case before preparing the contract for the client to sign and/or agreeing to what you need up front.

Years of experience will prove to you that crazy things happen, and you have to be prepared for the likely and the unlikely, even the ridiculous. I recall the first round of my first tournament in a law school mock trial, and the other side objected to leading on my cross examination. It took me a second to respond as I was not prepared for such an idiotic objection. For three months I had prepared approximately forty hours a week, and less than an hour into the tournament I had to deal with an objection I had no reason to even contemplate up until then.

Although an extreme example, you really need to be prepared for great counter attacks and foolish ones without being thrown off. Obviously, you should not spend a lot of valuable preparation time on pondering bad objections or arguments but when up against younger opponents you have to keep an eye out for mistakes that should not happen. During one jury trial the young prosecutor decided to ask the judge how she did on her jury selection right after it was completed. Although asking judges for their thoughts on performance after the trial is always a good idea, during the trial is an odd time to do it. The judge said she did a lot of good things and for whatever reason she asked the judge what he thought of my voir dire of the jury. The judge said that almost every single thing

I said was objectionable and she never objected. He said numerous times I delved into inappropriate yet not mistrial-worthy material and that once I saw I could get away with it without a prosecutor objection that I kept doing it even more. You can't prepare a case for times when you can get away with things that you should not of course, but you need to be ready to take advantage of things you never calculated. The work you put into the very first analysis of the case can determine how the next months or years of your life will go. Be sure you look at the case in an honest and clear fashion, so you know what to charge and you begin the process of managing client expectations from the very start.

II. Waging War

1. Sun Tzu said: In the operations of war, where there are in the field a thousand swift chariots, as many heavy chariots, and a hundred thousand mail-clad soldiers, with provisions enough to carry them a thousand li, the expenditure at home and at the front, including entertainment of guests, small items such as glue and paint, and sums spent on chariots and armor, will reach the total of a thousand ounces of silver per day. Such is the cost of raising an army of one hundred thousand men.

Costs are always a concern to a lawyer both from the standpoint of office supplies, office space etc. but also in the courtroom as well. When taking a case, a lawyer must anticipate costs of potential exhibits, demonstrative aids or expert witnesses to counter the scientific evidence and other material a state prosecutor or a well-funded company can produce. Without the proper tools for the argument, even a gifted lawyer will have difficulty arguing important points or against key opponent evidence. Ineffective calculations in the early stages of the case can plant the seed for defeat months or years before trial. Some law firms even take out bank loans to fund cases. Of course, this has additional risks and can affect the attorney as far as wanting to settle a case to recoup costs instead of going to trial and losing it all. You must be sure your needs don't conflict with your client's interests or preferences.

2. When you engage in actual fighting, if victory is long in coming, then men's weapons will grow dull, and their ardor will be damped. If you lay siege to a town, you will exhaust your strength.

You must remain sharp and ready. There is no unimportant part of litigation, no meaningless deposition or proceeding. Although some parts are more important than others, it is important to always be ready for any deposition or motion hearing, etc. It cannot be said with certainly that any particular matter won't be key at trial. That is why there are things called *surprises* after all, so pay careful attention for every step taken. There is no such thing as being too prepared or too mindful of the day's matters. Our profession is one that rewards preparation and severely punishes laziness. Shooting from the hip may be needed on occasion but it is not the most important skill for a successful lawyer to have.

3. Again, if the campaign is protracted, the resources of the State will not be equal to the strain.

The financial burden on a law office and the emotional strain on you as well as other lawyers on your team must be given attention. Everyone has highs and lows in spirit and strength. Issues at home, health issues or issues with your family may be exhausting your emotional resources as well. Cases can seem to rage like a fire with high heat for years but keeping focused is a keystone of any lawyer's performance. When on the job you must focus and not allow yourself to be distracted. Just like a fireman, if you take your eyes off of the mark you can be well and truly burned. You need to be mindful of your mental and physical health and take steps out of the office to stay at your best whether it be personal time, seeing a mental-health professional, or being sure to set aside time to focus on non-work-related concerns.

4. Now, when your weapons are dulled, your ardor damped, your strength exhausted and your treasure spent, other chieftains will spring up to take advantage of your extremity. Then no man, however wise, will be able to avert the consequences that must ensue.

It is foolish to think that you, or members of your team, will always be at their best and never make a mistake due to being worn down or other causes. It will happen, so don't be naïve or foolhardy to not at least see that it has occurred with hindsight. Acknowledge the error, chalk it up to a bad day, but don't ignore it. Do what you can to minimize the damage from it. When making a mistake in front of a jury, you certainly don't want the jury to know it, so don't bring attention to it by over-reacting.

5. Thus, though we have heard of stupid haste in war, cleverness has never been seen associated with long delays.

Delays are practically built into the litigation process. Even when the rules force things to go forward faster, as in criminal court, delays are constantly occurring. Delays should be expected, but never discount the fact that a judge may set early deadlines or trial dates ahead of what you may expect. You should not presume that even a lenient judge will always allow deadline extensions for filings or other key matters that may greatly impact a case. Having more time to prepare and get ready is always a plus that should not be wasted. Once your practice is in full swing, you should not seek to rush a case for the payoff, as hopefully you have enough cases open that, as they naturally settle or resolve, you will have a steady income stream.

6. There is no instance of a country having benefited from prolonged warfare.

Monetary budgets may be stretched to the limit, and that must always be a concern. It is key to not take a case that will consume you or your team from a financial standpoint or via other firm capacities. Also, a client, who is not as familiar with the system, may suffer from attrition far faster than the lawyer. Often the client's whole life is tied into whether they will lose millions of dollars or go to prison, etc. This may make them too eager to take a bad offer to resolve the case, so it is important to keep them up to speed as things progress and to *manage their expectations* as to when progress may be expected. To say a litigation should be done as fast possible is like saying that a particular snail is faster than you thought it would be. There is no way to truly make it go fast in the eyes of the client, so it is key to keep their expectations in line with what you believe to be a realistic timetable and to make them aware ahead of time what kinds of delays may be expected and why during the case. If you don't do this, you will also have to deal with a client who is constantly harassing you regarding the current status of the case.

7. It is only one who is thoroughly acquainted with the evils of war that can thoroughly understand the profitable way of carrying it on.

Although you may understand the long and protracted nature of war via litigation, the client usually does not. Even those who have some understating or experience may be even worse, as their prior cases may seem so much better to them as they do not understand the complexities of this case compared to their prior matters. For the client a little bit of knowledge or experience can be dangerous, as they may think they know how this case should be working, and it isn't. They may even simply Google it and use that as the basis for why you are taking too long or doing something wrong. You must teach them what to expect, so they can prepare. Practice depositions, for example, are good for the client to go through in a civil case, so they are mentally more ready for the experience. With more capable clients you should talk to them about common traps or tricks they may encounter, and what they should do. Don't overwhelm them with too much information, but always cover basics such as their ability to say they can't answer that question with just a yes or no answer, or that they can ask the attorney to ask a confusing question again if they are unsure of what they are saying. These types of concerns are always on their mind, and if you can put them more at ease on the parts they have to participate in, they will have less anxiety and be more willing to go at a slower pace overall that you believe will suit the case strategy.

8. The skillful soldier does not raise a second levy, neither are his supply-wagons loaded more than twice.

As a lawyer in business to make money, obviously you want to get as much revenue as possible. Especially with a cost-conscious client, you want to think ahead regarding future costs. In addition to legal skills, you have to be able to plan your budget. Most lawyers quote an initial fee or retainer that they hope will cover the case from start to finish. Depending on jurisdiction and the type of case, the court may order you to finish the case, whether you are getting paid or not. Most judges will not accept a withdrawal too close to trial, especially on a complex matter.

9. Bring war material with you from home, but forage on the enemy. Thus the army will have food enough for its needs.

Pass off costs to the opposition whenever you ethically can. It is not just an issue of profit for the firm, but also to avoid the effects of a long and protracted litigation. It can add up: if the other party orders transcripts first from depositions and you can order just condensed copies, etc. it may save resources in the long run. At the time it may seem like an insignificant cost, but you should always keep in mind the long game and the effects that becoming low on funds can have on doing what you feel you need to do later on in the case. There are grave dangers in letting your finances affect, or seem to affect, your recommendation to take an offer or fight on.

10. Poverty of the State exchequer causes an army to be maintained by contributions from a distance. Contributing to maintain an army at a distance causes the people to be impoverished.

Costs add up. Can depositions be done in town and not out of town? Can a local expert be used? An argument about venue may seem to be relatively insignificant but having things closer can save on costs for hotels for your team, not to mention you will likely know the local judge's proclivities, if it is one you are familiar with.

11. On the other hand, the proximity of an army causes prices to go up; and high prices cause the people's substance to be drained away.

Most clients will say they can pay you more as a case goes forward, but whether they are sincere or not, as time goes by, they may later claim that they can't afford more. Even an honest client may intend to pay you as planned, but they can lose their job or have other financial emergencies come up. Although a general may know the financial abilities of the state, certainly you will not be able to know the real financial capabilities of your clients. Having pending criminal charges, for example, may make a local business person who is your client start to lose business from the bad press. Although not convicted, news coverage can make their clients and friends run for cover, and they will not have access to more funds that they truly thought would have been there.

12. When their substance is drained away, the peasantry will be afflicted by heavy exactions.

The client's attitude may change with unexpected costs. You will need to manage expectations on costs well ahead of time, when possible, to keep the client relatively content. Like a general, the lawyer can be replaced relatively easily. If the client thinks extra costs or delays are due to you, they may consult a new lawyer who may be promising them unrealistic goals just to get them in the door. Just like a professional sports team in a funk, the easiest thing can seem to be to fire the manager.

13, 14. With this loss of substance and exhaustion of strength, the homes of the people will be stripped bare, and three-tenths of their income will be dissipated; while government expenses for broken chariots, worn-out horses, breastplates and helmets, bows and arrows, spears and shields, protective mantles, draught-oxen and heavy wagons, will amount to four-tenths of its total revenue.

Unfortunately, costs are important to litigation. The ability of some entities to have the benefit of limitless resources, such as the state in criminal matters or defendants who are large companies or insurance defense, etc. Dealing with opponents who have unlimited resources is a special challenge. Clearly, the deep pockets of an opponent can be attractive in a civil case, and in a criminal case there are constitutional and other protections that can be used to confront the state's massive resources, but special consideration must be taken on all decisions, as this factor can change almost every calculation. The law is supposed to allow for a fair and level playing field, but even a giant fighting with one arm tied behind their back can still present an uneven contest to a regular-sized individual.

15. Hence a wise general makes a point of foraging on the enemy. One cartload of the enemy's provisions is equivalent to twenty of one's own, and likewise a single picul of his provender is equivalent to twenty from one's own store.

Certainly, you should not try to steal your opponent's legal pads at a deposition or court hearing but as long as your witnesses are not intimidated, doing a deposition at their office or splitting costs on reporter or transcript costs can be significant savings and in the alternate pass on a cost to the opponent. Let them pay for the coffee and donuts.

16. Now, in order to kill the enemy, our men must be roused to anger; that there may be advantage from defeating the enemy, they must have their rewards.

Avoiding incarceration or receiving giant piles of money is always a great motivator. The tools to motivate the client are always present, but you must, of course, temper expectations toward realistic outcomes and rewards for the struggles to be endured. A client who has been wronged or hurt in an accident or a client who fears incarceration will be prepared to fight. They will expect a financial prize in a civil suit and maybe even a chance to sue if they are acquitted in a criminal case. You can also play on their emotions to motivate them to fight, if you think it is wise. Remind a criminal defendant that they should not have to take a plea to something they didn't do, or appealing to a civil client that they have been wronged and should have proper compensation for them or their family, etc.

17. Therefore in chariot fighting, when ten or more chariots have been taken, those should be rewarded who took the first. Our own flags should be substituted for those of the enemy, and the chariots mingled and used in conjunction with ours. The captured soldiers should be kindly treated and kept.

Most lawyers have help, either associate attorneys, partners or legal staff. Although the client is the State, your staff needs to be motivated as well. They will know when you have a big win and will always want a taste. Although the other lawyer's staff will not likely want to join your firm, you do need to keep your own staff happy for the wars to come, and when you want to recruit new lawyers or staff, some of your best applicants may be people that have seen you and your team in action and respect you enough to want to join you.

18. This is called, using the conquered foe to augment one's own strength.

What is the source of your team's motivations? If one particular employee finds a key piece of evidence in a mountain of discovery, reward them. Although infighting and competition can lead to problems, rewards and even just praise can motivate your team members to go a little bit further or a little bit faster.

19. In war, then, let your great object be victory, not lengthy campaigns.

Billable hours aside, you can't lose sight of the ultimate goal, be it an acquittal, a large monetary judgement, or the successful defense of a suit. On flat-fee matters this is always clear, but you have to keep in mind the old saying that a colleague of mine often cited to "that pigs get fat and hogs get slaughtered". It is best to not prolong a case due to greed only to have missed a great settlement window and have a case later unravel. Many sure-things and can't-miss cases have developed fatal flaws that would have not been visible under the most detailed review earlier.

20. Thus it may be known that the leader of armies is the arbiter of the people's fate, the man on whom it depends whether the nation shall be in peace or in peril.

Any general has had preferences or personal objectives to bring forward their own notoriety or prestige with a nation's leaders. The client will only judge you based on their notion of winning or losing, i.e., money or avoiding jail, etc. Some lawyers may become distracted by the lure and attraction of what media attention can do for your practice. You must always make decisions with the client in mind and not other fringe benefits you may gain from their case. Most state bars allow posting notices of wins on your website, etc. as long as the names are not mentioned, and the always-present happy client, sharing your name as they brag, will hopefully bring your practice growth and more success. You should also ask a very happy client to give you a Google review etc as potential new clients pay close attention to such things.

III. Attack by Stratagem

1. Sun Tzu said: In the practical art of war, the best thing of all is to take the enemy's country whole and intact; to shatter and destroy it is not so good. So, too, it is better to recapture an army entire than to destroy it, to capture a regiment, a detachment or a company entire than to destroy them.

Of course, one law firm can't capture another, although from time to time their employees may switch, or better still, a client may move over for future litigation. It is true for all that, if you capture an opposing army without a fight, as you strategically put yourself in such an advantageous position that they felt they had to yield, it will cost you far fewer casualties. The fight for a lawyer does not start at trial; it starts the very first moment you take the case. Opportunities like depositions can be chances for you to show the opponent that their position is untenable, and they should settle, etc. Especially in cases where you are paid a percentage and not hourly, it is important to bring the other side down with as little expenditure of your own resources as possible. You should also not ignore a free advantage.

Although you must prepare for the best lawyer possible to be your opponent, you should not overlook a young lawyer who may surrender a point they should not. I have had an assistant attorney general concede a stipulation at an oral argument that was key to my success. I have had prosecutors who are lazy or ignorant agree to foundation or other items that would have been great attack points if they had seen it. It also costs nothing to check with an opponent to see if they will give you something that can make your life easier. Sometimes they won't see its significance and sometimes they may offer you something, if you counter with something else to give back, that doesn't harm your standing. Although litigation is often a nasty and contentious process, you should not pass up a chance to make things a bit easier or less costly for yourself.

2. Hence to fight and conquer in all your battles is not supreme excellence; supreme excellence consists in breaking the enemy's resistance without fighting.

The goal in litigation is to win, not to fight and win. Often actions can be taken early on to show that the 'fight' at trial will not bear fruit for the other side, and they should cut their losses now. The best lawyer is not the one who wins one hundred trials with no losses. Juries can be strange and find against you for reasons that make no sense. The goal is to avoid such a possibility *and* still get your client exactly what they want, or more realistically, so much that they think trial is not worth the risk. 'Winning', whether it means you get paid or your client avoids jail or some other goal, is the sought-after prize or measurement of success. Will your client really care if you won a jury trial to get him acquitted of serious criminal charges vs you filing a motion to suppress that forces the state to dismiss? Will they care if you use a technicality to obtain a million-dollar settlement offer? They will not, and neither should you. Just as a country's leader determines the goals for a war, so too does the client set the bar for victory.

3. Thus the highest form of generalship is to balk the enemy's plans; the next best is to prevent the junction of the enemy's forces; the next in order is to attack the enemy's army in the field; and the worst policy of all is to besiege walled cities.

There are numerous benefits to getting your opponent to waste time and have to delay what they later find is to be a necessary step. Delays can cost more money for them; it can affect morale and confidence in the opposition team or client, or numerous other issues. Any kind of disruption you can cause your opponent, that does not unduly cost you, is well worth it. You may have to engage the opposition, but it is important to only do so on as advantageous or at least level a position as possible.

4. The rule is, not to besiege walled cities if it can possibly be avoided. The preparation of mantlets, movable shelters, and various implements of war, will take up three whole months; and the piling up of mounds over against the walls will take three months more.

The same holds true for lawyers in that you want to avoid attacking a well-entrenched enemy if you can, especially one that is nestled inside their 'fortifications'. A corporate client is best fought out of their preferred jurisdiction if you can get the venue moved. If a criminal case can be moved to another county, do it. Let the prosecutor have to travel and not be able to work as much out of the comforts of their office. Let them face a jury with a different makeup then they are used to, urban vs rural for example; let them deal with a judge they don't see on a regular basis or play golf with or went to law school together.

5. The general, unable to control his irritation, will launch his men to the assault like swarming ants, with the result that one-third of his men are slain, while the town still remains untaken. Such are the disastrous effects of a siege.

So often have lawyers proceeded with a trial as they had their feathers ruffled at some point. On the grand scale numerous lawyers have let themselves be controlled by their emotions and it affected their encouragement to the client to go to trial or a prosecutor sought to avoid negative media attention by not dismissing a case only to be draped with media attention over a not guilty verdict and claims of wasting taxpayer dollars. At the tactical level many lawyers have asked the dreaded one question to many, and it has cost them dearly.

Every lawyer has heard of a case where, for example, the lawyer is pointing out the flaws in the critical eyewitness testimony; noting that it was dark, that they were not wearing their glasses and that the witness had been at an odd angle to see the scene when an alleged assault took place only to continue on with just one more question and to have the witness say something like "well no they didn't see the assault but when I moved closer, they were the only two people there and he threw down the bat that had blood on it" etc. The most notorious example of this rule being violated is the witness who is broken down and finally concedes they did not see the defendant bite the hand of the victim, only to be followed with the one too many question of "well then how do you know it was the Defendant? To which they retort with "because I saw the defendant spit out a finger." A less extreme answer may simply be a good witness who, after a long and successful pocket of questions, points out visual hindrances etc., says something along the lines of "no, it was the most horrible thing I have ever seen in my life; I will never forget it."

6. Therefore the skillful leader subdues the enemy's troops without any fighting; he captures their cities without laying siege to them; he overthrows their kingdom without lengthy operations in the field.

Ideally a lawyer can do the same. It is limited, of course, but you have to keep in mind that the finish line of any litigation is to get what your client wants or what they think is a win. Just like the relationship between the politician and the general, the client-to-the lawyer relationship sets the victory point. Getting to that point without going through unneeded work or hearings and depositions is a goal the lawyer should target. However, you get to the point where your client-is-happy is the best goal. To get there as fast as possible without compromising your chances of success, especially on contingency or flat fee cases, is the bullseye of your aim. Unless you do hourly billing, there is no reason to waste time or effort unless you think you can out-spend a smaller opponent. Extra battles and dragging yourself through mud with no gain toward that bullseye is something to avoid.

7. **With his forces intact he will dispute the mastery of the Empire, and thus, without losing a man, his triumph will be complete. This is the method of attacking by stratagem.**

There are always ways to get an opponent to a point when they know that the ultimate disposition of the case is inevitable. Once you achieve that then you can get an opponent to settle or reach your victory point without further unneeded litigation cost or risk. The opposition's client must be put in a place to tell their lawyer that they don't want to fight anymore as they know it will be a waste of money or they want the pain of the struggle to go away so they can finally move on. Of course, you can't talk directly to the opposition client and the opposing lawyer may misinform their client, but you do what you can to make your position of strength known to the opposition.

When I was a prosecutor, I had a defense lawyer who kept filing and arguing clearly baseless motions to suppress evidence that really were just a chance for him to rattle his saber in front of his client, presumably to justify his fees. For that lawyer I started only noting case law against his points, that were cases he himself had argued in the appellate courts. I would point out that I was shocked he still thought X, Y, or Z were true as he himself had already argued these points to the higher court, *and lost*. He quickly stopped filing these frivolous motions to impress his client as his clients were coming away with the very opposite opinion of his work on their behalf. This enabled me to "win" future cases that I would have had to have fought without having to fight at all.

8. It is the rule in war, if our forces are ten to the enemy's one, to surround him; if five to one, to attack him; if twice as numerous, to divide our army into two.

Although a rare luxury for most, it is important to know how to handle the high ground or other advantage that gives you the better position or advantages. Best is to show the force without betraying any weakness to make the opposition call it a day and cut their losses. You also don't want to delay and have your position weaken so it is key to review accurately your strengths and weaknesses and how stable they are, to decide if you and when you should attack.

Underdogs can win. Things can always go wrong. A previously strong witness can wither or make a mistake at a deposition that effects their credibility etc. Once you commit to a fight you can't proceed halfheartedly. For a lawyer the right answer to this is always with the client. You must give them the pros and cons and be sure to spell in out in writing. By doing so you can say it was their informed decision if things go wrong to no fault of your own. You can say that you mapped it all out for them and they made their choice with full awareness of all the relevant material. They will also ask you what the right way forward is, and they may insist that you tell them as you are the expert so you must give them direction. Whenever possible give them a clear picture of the layout but make it so they make the final decision.

9. If equally matched, we can offer battle; if slightly inferior in numbers, we can avoid the enemy; if quite unequal in every way, we can flee from him.

You can only run for so long in the court process. If you don't have a good offer, and you don't have the strength to frighten the opposition into submission, then you must prepare both yourself and your client for a hard fight. Again, managing expectations is key, but this is the time when the lawyer's true skill will be tested. Every lawyer or judge has a story about a jury that they were sure would go one way and went the other. Jurors are always the measure of the win or loss. The lawyer must analyze each case to gauge accurately what your position is and what options you have. Sometimes you have to lay it out to a client in such a way that communicates they have to take a deal they may not want, even though it is in their best interest to take it. The exact parameters for knowing a case and being able to analyze it to the point where you will know a correct assessment of your situation and whether you should fight or flee, can be largely guided by a handful of things. The laws of your jurisdiction, the facts of the case, your understanding of the relevant case, particular factors, and a three-thousand-year-old text on war written by a man in China.

10. Hence, though an obstinate fight may be made by a small force, in the end it must be captured by the larger force.

A small force may be deployed solely with an intent not to win a battle or take and hold an objective, but rather to drain the opponent's forces. A small force may draw a substantial amount of the opposition to force them out of their reserve or counter them in some other way. In the context of law there can be times when a small opponent attacks a larger force like a rabid dog, such as the state in a criminal case. In this context, a smaller force may press an unrealistic attack with the hope that the resource drain on the opposition will be too much, i.e., the state won't want to waste time with a smaller case as they should spend their resources on a larger matter etc. It can arise in a civil context that the expenditure involved, for example, to travel to many different places for very short depositions may add to the presumed cost for the larger side, and they may choose a plea option simply to avoid litigation costs that may end up costing more than the settlement itself of what would be a can't-lose case for them.

11. Now the general is the bulwark of the State; if the bulwark is complete at all points; the State will be strong; if the bulwark is defective, the State will be weak.

There is no such thing as an army or state that is strong enough to continuously endure a foolish general. There have been generals over the years who have obtained their rank due to politics or other connections and not based on merit. They lead their state to death and destruction. Similarly, there are lawyers who obtain their positions and reputation based on falsities or connections and not on merit. There are even lawyers who can't pass the Bar and have to seek a waiver for admission. This holds true in other professions, such as for doctors, police officers, and teachers, etc. Just because you have a law license does not mean that you have no flaws. You must compensate for them and be aware of them to ensure that you don't sink an otherwise unsinkable ship. There is no such thing as a good lawyer who thinks they are without flaws.

12. There are three ways in which a ruler can bring misfortune upon his army:

13. (1) By commanding the army to advance or to retreat, being ignorant of the fact that it cannot obey. This is called hobbling the army.

To a large degree this should only happen if the lawyer has not done a good job of managing expectations with the client and making sure they trust you to run the case. There are always going to be cases when a client snaps and instructs the lawyer to take a plea deal or a settlement, even if the lawyer thinks a better deal can be obtained if they stay the course. The law requires that we listen to the client but we must be ready to deliver a convincing argument to the client of their mistake if we believe the landscape of the case indicates it.

The client may also seek a path forward that is unrealistic or unattainable. Managing client expectations from day one is a key part of the representation, so that they are not blinded by the dream of a huge payout for a small case, etc. You don't want a client demanding a trial or fight in some other way when you know the odds are stacked against you. You should never promise the client some level of success up front just to get them signed up as a client. When you first meet with them, you have to start managing expectations, and you can't know the true strength of the case before the discovery process.

14. (2) By attempting to govern an army in the same way as he administers a kingdom, being ignorant of the conditions which obtain in an army. This causes restlessness in the soldier's minds.

A client needs to learn the ins and outs of the process. We forget, after working in the legal system for years, how it may seem to others who are completely new to the process. We have to be careful to make sure from the onset that the client knows it will be a lengthy and often slow-moving struggle. We must advise them ahead of time to expect delays, so they don't think we were simply unprepared or not acting appropriately.

Even worse than in other professions is the flood of television and movie representations of our profession that has led to a fanciful view of how the process really works. Law and Order episodes are always over in an hour or two and still find a way to squeeze in profitable commercials to boot. Meanwhile, a real client may learn all too harshly that they won't make bail on a capital case or that the specter of a pending criminal or civil matter may be something that will live with them for years as the case progresses agonizingly slow. We must appreciate the difficulty in the client not knowing how their case will impact them in the days and weeks ahead or for the rest of their life. The impact on their life can all be based on the outcome of your work, for better or worse.

15. (3) By employing the officers of his army without discrimination, through ignorance of the military principle of adaptation to circumstances. This shakes the confidence of the soldiers.

On criminal matters a client or their family may seek out a second opinion from a trusted family-law attorney or someone else they know. In a civil case a client may have in house counsel or other internal staff that may affect the judgment of their leader with misleading information. Many times, a client is a multi-teared organization or a person whose family is pulling them in several directions. We must know this and deal with it during the pendency of the case.

Most lawyers will also have other lawyers or staff on their team. You have to be mindful of their morale and how they adapt to changes. You want to make sure newer members of the team know of possible issues and are not distracted or greatly alarmed by developments. They may communicate their perceived distress to the client. They may also grow afraid that their hoped-for bonus or promotion is in jeopardy, if the case fails. The client and your team will look to you as a barometer to measure the damage from an unexpected turn, so be sure not to overreact.

16. But when the army is restless and distrustful, trouble is sure to come from the other feudal princes. This is simply bringing anarchy into the army and flinging victory away.

Trust is key and a two-way street. To a degree we have to trust the client. Not only that they trust us, but we must trust them to give us accurate information, especially when key material, that we need to properly gauge the lay of the land before us, comes from them.

When your team second guesses your choices or questions your leadership, then the disarray can lead to infighting or other consequences for the case or for your whole practice. They must feel they have a way to voice their strategic concerns to you. It costs nothing to listen to them, and they may even be right.

17. Thus we may know that there are five essentials for victory: (1) He will win who knows when to fight and when not to fight. (2) He will win who knows how to handle both superior and inferior forces. (3) He will win whose army is animated by the same spirit throughout all its ranks. (4) He will win who, prepared himself, waits to take the enemy unprepared. (5) He will win who has military capacity and is not interfered with by the sovereign.

This all holds true for the lawyer. As so often is the case, in life you need to know when to fight and when to stall and wait for more advantageous conditions. As Kenny Rogers said "you have to know when to hold them and know when to fold them." You must know how to properly handle situations where you have an advantage or a superior position or when you have to take advantage of opportunities to have even a chance to win. You have to keep your troops and your client on the same page as yourself to keep their spirit up without getting them to think they have a great chance when they don't, etc. You must prepare with all possible tools available to you to maximize your chances. It is up to you to make sure that your team is as prepared as possible at any given moment and for every hearing, deposition, or meeting with a witness. You often can only control how ready you are. You certainly can't make an opponent be lazy, but you can be ready and use an advantage when you see an opening that requires being able to mobilize at the right time. You have to make sure the client doesn't interfere with what is best, even though they do, like a king or queen, have the legal right to make a final decision in the end.

18. Hence the saying: If you know the enemy and know yourself, you need not fear the result of a hundred battles. If you know yourself but not the enemy, for every victory gained you will also suffer a defeat. If you know neither the enemy nor yourself, you will succumb in every battle.

Know what you can do and what you can't. Know what your team is capable of and what they are not. Know your weakness and your strengths. You have to know what you excel at and what you are likely to struggle with. Every lawyer is different, just like every general. All have strengths and weaknesses. You need to learn what you can about your opposition, know what kind of firm they are, and what resources they do or don't have. You need to know if the prosecutor assigned to the case is a lazy coaster or ambitious and likes to fight, etc. Knowing the players as well as the terrain, such as the judge, is key to decisions you will need to make as the case goes along, and you may need that material available ahead of time so you can make split-second decisions that necessity may force you into.

IV. Tactical Dispositions

1. Sun Tzu said: The good fighters of old first put themselves beyond the possibility of defeat, and then waited for an opportunity of defeating the enemy.

More often than you would think the fight is decided by a mistake or miscalculation. Your opponent will likely make one, but the key is to notice it, and be able to exploit it. Of course, you must do all you can to avoid an error on your side as well. If you made one, then you can't let it get to you while you do your best to protect yourself. In modern times, a lawyer is only as skilled as they are at the moment, they take a case. You can spend time applying your skills and learn what you can from cases as they occur but, in the end, the best thing you can do to put you and your client in the best possible position is to prepare, prepare, and prepare some more.

2. To secure ourselves against defeat lies in our own hands, but the opportunity of defeating the enemy is provided by the enemy himself.

A prosecutor builds their case, and they always include unintended flaws and weak points which the defense lawyer must find and exploit. The State will not intentionally broadcast their case's flaws. It is up to the defense to protect their week points while always searching for the possible flaws in the State's case. For the state, the defendant who may bungle a key aspect of a crime, may seal their own fate for the case by gifting the state an easy evidence issue that is key to success. There is little you can do about what a client does before they come to you, but it is wise to tell future clients that you prefer to help them avoid problems, instead of fixing those that have already occurred. Being charged with a crime or being served with a lawsuit is not the time to talk to a lawyer; it is long before that.

3. Thus the good fighter is able to secure himself against defeat, but cannot make certain of defeating the enemy.

All you can do is prepare yourself, your client, and your team for the fight. There can be instances where you lose a case, as the facts and circumstances or even luck line up against you. You can never be *certain* of an outcome and should never guarantee one, no matter how good a case looks at any point. You can prepare yourself for the coming fight, to the best of your ability, but you can't be certain if it will be enough. How well the other side's case is prepared is a factor that you can rarely alter.

4. Hence the saying: One may know how to conquer without being able to do it.

You may be able to prepare yourself to the absolute best that you know but it may not be enough. You should always do everything you can to prepare, and yet you may still believe the loss is inevitable. If the client wants to continue in spite of the odds or through desperation, all you can do is to ready yourself. There may be things that you could do to win but they are beyond you or not within the bounds of the rules. In the most desperate of situations be it war or the specter of facing prison for a client, people will insist that they must fight. As such you

46

have to learn to prepare for fights that you will almost certainly lose. The profession of law is rare in that regard. Never find yourself in a position where after a case is over, you wonder what if you had done something more. Losing a case can happen, losing a case as you did not do enough to win, will and should, haunt you forever.

5. Security against defeat implies defensive tactics; ability to defeat the enemy means taking the offensive.

There is usually a time for both, given the surrounding circumstances. As in war, it is often difficult to engage in an offensive without having your defenses in order. You don't want to leave yourself open to an attack at a weak point but if you choose to attack, the force must be strong enough to accomplish its objective. In war you can leave behind a force to hold a key point. In a case you have to simultaneously prepare for your attack and break down the other sides' witness(es) and evidence while boosting your own witnesses and protecting them from their own flaws. You *will* have flaws in your case, and you must spend an appropriate amount of time preparing to minimize them. Though not as fun or glorious as preparing for a punishing and memorable attack, defense is essential to winning. In basketball for example we all love to watch replays of a great Bam Adebayo dunk or a Caitlin Clark logo three-point shot, but when the game is over it is hard not to notice that the team that lost by only a few points also missed a few boring free throws.

6. Standing on the defensive indicates insufficient strength; attacking, a superabundance of strength.

It's important to be able to properly analyze your own case to determine what strength you really have. Knowing to go forward or circle the wagons, is a key skill. It is also one that you must not allow your ego to distort.

7. The general who is skilled in defense hides in the most secret recesses of the earth; he who is skilled in attack flashes forth from the topmost heights of heaven. Thus, on the one hand we have ability to protect ourselves; on the other, a victory that is complete.

The art of being a lawyer is at the forefront when you have to show the strength of your case and your team to your opponent, in the hope that they take a deal that *you* want while at the same time not giving away too much information, so that the opponents don't know how you are going to attack them if you go to trial. You have to disclose some strategy but hold back on exact tactics. All the while you have to comply with the discovery process and disclose certain mandatory materials. The precise and delicate balance needed with this is key. You want to keep your plans for attack well-hidden until you draw your opponents out in a key cross, etc. Although you don't want to seem vulnerable, you still need to hold ways to defend your key points in reserve so that your opponent can't fully prepare a way to break your defense down.

8. To see victory only when it is within the ken of the common herd is not the acme of excellence.

Looking at a case and properly advising or deciding how to go forward based on that analysis is a cornerstone of your practice. Seeing that a case is a slam dunk case (if there is such a thing) is no test of skill. It is seeing the way to win the close contest or pulling off the long-shot win that is the mark of an accomplished professional. A victory may be contingent on a lengthy string of dominos dependent on each of the previous ones to fall in the right way and at the precise time that you need them to. Hindsight is 20/20 but only the best litigator can see the lay of the land miles and months down the road.

9. Neither is it the acme of excellence if you fight and conquer and the whole Empire says, "Well done!"

Remember wining a great battle with personal honor or glory is not the goal. The goal is to get the win for the client while avoiding risk to them as much as possible.

10. To lift an autumn hair is no sign of great strength; to see the sun and moon is no sign of sharp sight; to hear the noise of thunder is no sign of a quick ear.

Winning a very strong case is no proof of great skill. The blind squirrel can still find a nut. Lighting up a brand-new officer on cross may be good for a case but it is no sign of ability. Of course, preparing for the weak witness as if they may be strong is the best practice, as they may be an untested opponent who could surprise you if you are not ready.

11. What the ancients called a clever fighter is one who not only wins but excels in winning with ease.

If you are doing it correctly, no case should be *easy*, as you should always prepare to the fullest. Certainly, looking like you won with ease is good, as you can let others you may face in the future think that you are skilled. However, never believe that you can win with ease; don't ever let victories get to your head and cloud you for future battles. A jury trial over a traffic ticket is still a jury trial and should be treated as such. Winning a case that makes you look like you brought it home with a slam dunk is valuable. While you must do all you can to win a case, there is something to be said for not wasting resources of your client or your firm. It is hard to balance the needs of your time or your firm's resources with making sure enough work has been done to win the case. Often it is the prep that makes the win seem to be easy. Abraham Lincoln is credited with saying that "If you give me six hours to chop down a tree I will spend the first four sharpening my axe."

12. Hence his victories bring him neither reputation for wisdom nor credit for courage.

In the age of the internet, it is normal for a lawyer to note their wins on their websites as news or testimonials, etc. Every client is afraid and wants to know if you are a 'winner' or not. It is not wrong to spark confidence in your client, but every case is won or lost based on its own particulars.

13. He wins his battles by making no mistakes. Making no mistakes is what establishes the certainty of victory, for it means conquering an enemy that is already defeated.

There is no such thing as preparing too much for a case. There will always be variables and aspects that are out of your control. The only thing you can do is prepare, prepare, prepare. This does not mean worthless repetitiveness but going over every aspect that you can think of and pondering every situation that may arise and what you would do in response.

14. Hence the skillful fighter puts himself into a position which makes defeat impossible and does not miss the moment for defeating the enemy.

Defeat is always possible. The variable of a jury will always be present, and they can always break against the ebb-and-flow of evidence. The only way to maximize your chances in every fight is to put yourself in the best position possible. You have to prepare for every possibility you can think of both from a tactical and a strategic level. The more you prepare, the faster your reaction will be in the heat of the critical moment. The window is always small to lock in an opponent witness in a trap or parry a counter from the opposition as if you knew it was coming. In Zen Buddhism, repetition and preparedness can lead to much faster action. A horse-mounted archer continuously adjusts to the changing wind, the horse's steps and shifts, and variations in the ground they ride on, yet the best one can hit a small bullseye time after time. They can do that because they have trained their minds to do it practically without thought. Just as we walk down the street without thinking at all about the steps we take or the shifts in the sidewalk, you must be sure in the courtroom of your actions as much as you would be while walking around in your backyard.

15. Thus it is that in war the victorious strategist only seeks battle after the victory has been won, whereas he who is destined to defeat, first fights and afterwards looks for victory.

If you are prepared to meet all attacks ahead of time, you maximize your chances of winning. Whether it is a lone deposition or the trial itself, you need to walk into the room ready in every way you can, as that is the best way to 'seek battle'. You should only go to trial after all the necessary preparation steps are ready and have been meticulously lined up. Going to trial in the hopes that things will break your way is a foolish way to proceed. No one has a crystal ball to predict what will happen, and there will always be surprises, but many steps must be prepared before trial, so they can be presented at trial effectively. In the modern world, the jury will want and demand that they be shown evidence in a way they are familiar, i.e., audio-visual whenever possible, such as enlarged maps or charts or video displayed on a screen large enough for the jury to take in the key material. You must prepare ahead of time to have the right witnesses and an exhibit lined up. You have to have gone over your material with your witnesses to make sure they respond to your questions as planned. You can't feed a witness a question or answer, but in most jurisdictions, you can present questions to them and see how they respond ahead of time, then adjust accordingly. You must have your cross material pre-planned in outline form if you want to keep a better flow than what might occur with pre-typed questions; however, you must still have at the ready what you plan to use for impeachment, such as clean copies of reports and depositions that you will present as needed for an impeachment purposes. Your ability to adjust to a surprise may very well save the day and lead to a moment you later share with colleagues, but if you are not fully prepared, your cause will be lost regardless of how well you shoot from the hip.

Also, keep in mind that even the old-west gunfighter who would literally shoot from the hip, had to prepare and practice to be able to use that skill in a life-or-death situation. It is something of a misnomer to think that anyone can shoot from the hip without first preparing to do so. Your ability to do so in trial will be amplified greatly by your level of preparedness.

16. The consummate leader cultivates the moral law, and strictly adheres to method and discipline; thus, it is in his power to control success.

Many generals or lawyers and, for that matter, pro athletes, politicians, doctors, etc. will fail at a critical moment in their careers due to not following the path of a 'professional'. Screwing around and not paying attention to detail or doing everything you can to prepare for every phase and moment of the battle can and will come back to haunt you. Having too many drinks the night before trial or anything else that keeps you from being your best is an inexcusable violation of your legal oath and moral obligations to your client and yourself.

17. In respect of military method, we have, firstly, Measurement; secondly, Estimation of quantity; thirdly, Calculation; fourthly, Balancing of chances; fifthly, Victory.

18. Measurement owes its existence to Earth; Estimation of quantity to Measurement; Calculation to Estimation of quantity; Balancing of chances to Calculation; and Victory to Balancing of chances.

1 Measurement—

The lay of the land is often the best place to start when analyzing a case. What natural advantages are there for your side and theirs? For example, certain kinds of witness have a natural credibility or lack thereof. There are many examples such as the old example of a reverend vs a prostitute, an older eyewitness vs a younger one, a witness with a criminal history vs a neutral and detached third-party witness, etc. Like in war there can also be 'the high ground'. Emotional witnesses (such as the victim in a domestic assault or a disabled victim in a automobile-accident case) can be a natural 'high ground' that by their mere existence and being observed by the jury are helpful to the case. A sympathetic child or crying victim will always have some natural protection of sympathy from the jury when facing tough cross questions. They of course can still be taken with an overwhelming number of facts delivered in a calculated fashion, but such natural advantages or disadvantages have to be reviewed from a tactical and strategic estimation in order to make proper calculations regarding predicted chances at trial.

Witness are not just names on a police report. I once had a domestic-assault trial where the victim was a month into her pregnancy but by the time of trial, she was weeks away from delivery. You have to make the decision if you can't move the trial again to try to ignore the pregnancy as irrelevant or note in front of the jury how far along she is now vs when the alleged assault occurred or if the pregnancy was even known at the time, etc. You may choose just to let it lay but then you can get jurors who are less intelligent to be unsure of what her condition was at the time of the assault. The more you talk about her pregnancy, of course, the more time you are spending on what is a sympathetic condition to many jurors.

2 Estimation of quantity–

Never to be confused with quality, quantity can still be an impressive and impactive factor. In a complex prosecution, for example, having a sheer volume of witnesses or, in an assault case, having several eyewitnesses, is going to weigh on the jury, regardless of the criminal history of one or the eyesight of another; the jury may see them as too many witnesses for all of them to be wrong. It may be hard to question how a half-dozen witnesses or multiple doctors, etc. could all possibly have been mistaken. A prosecutor having four eyewitnesses to a crime when all of them are high on methamphetamine is an example of quantity not having value due to a lack of quality.

3 Calculation–

This comes from not only looking at the size of the force against you but the quality and other factors. You must analyze the case as you think it will be and as it may be. Will key evidence get limined out? Will a key witness hold up or will they crack under the pressure of the moment in front of the jury? What can you promise in opening remarks without risking being seen as a liar? Will a certain order of witnesses affect your ability to show foundation for an exhibit or not? These kinds of matters must be thoroughly reviewed in trial preparation.

4 Balancing of Chances–

There are always variables such as the largess of the jury. Also, when analyzing the admissibility of key evidence such as: will the excited utterance of a non-present alleged victim be admissible against hearsay objections be determined by the judge as much or more so than by case law? The judge is to follow the law, but the law is always up for interpretation. Most of the rulings issued by the United States Supreme Court, after all, have been split decisions. The members of the Supreme Court are the best of the best of our jurists, and yet they disagree on almost every case. As such, a local judge may be swayed by their natural proclivities in how they view the law. Even in jurisdictions when a judge is supposed to be above party politics, they will still know one lawyer better than the other or have had a bad experience with a lawyer that may taint their rulings to your benefit or detriment, if you are that lawyer. They also have natural human tendencies like everyone else, where they lean toward a more liberal or conservative stance. To properly measure chances, one key aspect is what you can expect from key evidentiary rulings.

5 Victory—

This can only be estimated by a close look at all of these factors combined. Victory can't and should never be guaranteed to the client, but there will always be a time when the client asks what their chances are. The carefully crafted answer to this must always be presented to a client in a way they can understand while also taking into consideration complex factors that they may not even fully comprehend.

19. A victorious army opposed to a routed one, is as a pound's weight placed in the scale against a single grain.

To face an opponent who is not following the rules in this guide and controlling the facts of their case is doomed to failure. Although a lawyer must never underestimate their opponent, it can be seen before the trial is over that your strength appears to be overwhelming. While the pleasure of victory can be appreciated, it should not be a reason to ever take your foot off the gas.

20. The onrush of a conquering force is like the bursting of pent-up waters into a chasm a thousand fathoms deep.

As is the case with rushing waters, the power of the flow cannot be re-routed, so you must be sure the force is aimed at the target. Once set in motion, often you can do nothing but ride the waves as you are locked into what you promised in the opening statement.

V. Energy

1. Sun Tzu said: The control of a large force is the same principle as the control of a few men: it is merely a question of dividing up their numbers.

You must break down your opponent's witnesses, as they are often the bedrock of the case. If you have complex litigation or you are a prosecutor heading up a team of assistant DAs, you will need to manage the workload of your staff and lawyers. You must keep in mind the experience and vision of your assisting attorneys when deciding which tasks to delegate or to even delegate a particular task at all. You will need to decide what to delegate to support staff as well. Even if you are on a case by yourself, you only have so much time to give to any one case. You must wisely decide what facets need more attention than others. As in war, the troops you send out on a mission may be far away and difficult if not impossible to observe as they seek to carry out your orders. Their ability to function without you looking over their shoulders, will be a key factor to what you decide they can be trusted with.

2. Fighting with a large army under your command is no ways different from fighting with a small one: it is merely a question of instituting signs and signals.

In the modern world we have the ability to efficiently and quickly communicate with one another and, of course, to keep a record of those communications for any future use. Even during a court proceeding the practice of writing a note on a legal pad can now be done via email or text message or internal group messaging. Technology, when working correctly, in law as in war can be a fantastic tool to communicate strike points or other key data with unprecedented speeds and efficiency. For example, when offering an impeachment, the assisting attorney should know ahead of time what part of a deposition to pull up so that the trial attorney can impeach as needed, with no gap in time to execute the impeachment. Impeachments must be quick and precise to be effective and to stick with the jury.

3. To ensure that your whole host may withstand the brunt of the enemy's attack and remain unshaken—this is affected by maneuvers direct and indirect.

There will be some hits that your team must take, and you may know in general when they are coming. Softening the blows is critical. If you have a witness who offers solid help to your case but has a prior crime of dishonesty with which they will be impeached on cross, then it is often best to bring it up and explain it yourself instead of waiting for the opposition to milk the point with zeal on *their* cross. You must be at the ready for the rehabilitation of a witness on re-direct or an efficient and memorable lightning strike of a cross or re-cross. Fair or unfair, even though we know the court process can be slow and boring, the jury has been inundated with tv shows and movies like *A Few Good Men* or *Suits* where they expect a quick and dramatic back-and-forth pace. You can't always provide that, but it is always worth a try. Having a great strike of a cross question may go unnoticed if buried in the middle of an hour-long cross. Primacy and recency are still the standard-bearers to keep the Jury's limited attention, so you ought to bring a key point at the start or end.

Also, offering pauses or a change in volume of your voice for emphasis is still the right thing to do in a world where people are used to TikTok videos and other small-dose mediums.

4. **That the impact of your army may be like a grindstone dashed against an egg–this is effected by the science of weak points and strong.**

Long before the trial, the litigants must find the weak points of the case as a whole (strategic) and the weakness of each witness or element to be proven (tactical). To bring the weight of a flaw to bear at trial, you must be ready ahead of time to deliver the key strikes at times and in ways in which they will stay with the jury that registers them. You will want to touch on these matters as often as you can in closing and with other witnesses to makes sure they stick. Also, you must try to use them in closing via a visual medium whenever you can. We live in such a technological age that, with the assistance of technology, quick snippets of a video or audio clip to let the jury hear a key statement from a police video etc. is key to ensuring that you have the best chance that it sticks in the jury's mind especially during what could be a long deliberation by the jurors. For those of us who pride ourselves on our skills at oration, we can't be so arrogant not to note that in the modern world people are used to receiving their information through modern media.

5. **In all fighting, the direct method may be used for joining battle, but indirect methods will be needed in order to secure victory.**

Many witnesses, like officers and doctors, can have prior experience with giving testimony. Never underestimate a witness' ability to see what you are trying to do or what you are aiming toward with them. To take the witnesses down, you must take great care to lay out paths they can't diverge from. Using police reports, 911 calls, depositions, and other tools to know how to steer witnesses will be key. Don't generally expect the Perry-Mason moment. Sometimes it is enough to get small facts from multiple witnesses and then tie them together in closing.

6. Indirect tactics, efficiently applied, are inexhaustible as Heaven and Earth, unending as the flow of rivers and streams; like the sun and moon, they end but to begin anew; like the four seasons, they pass away to return once more.

There are many exhaustible resources. Your willingness to prepare is not one of them. You should see the case well enough to prepare both for the important points and for the key moments. You must spend the time preparing, and preparing well, so that you are ready to handle surprises as well as developing points with meticulous detail. On the morning of trial, when you look in the mirror, there is nothing you can do to be smarter or more personable. You need to be able to honestly say to yourself that you did all that can be done to prepare. Being fully prepared and ready is one of the few things you can completely control that can always increase your chances of success.

7. There are not more than five musical notes, yet the combinations of these five give rise to more melodies than can ever be heard.

8. There are not more than five primary colors (blue, yellow, red, white, and black), yet in combination they produce more hues than can ever been seen.

9. There are not more than five cardinal tastes (sour, acrid, salt, sweet, bitter), yet combinations of them yield more flavors than can ever be tasted.

10. In battle, there are not more than two methods of attack— the direct and the indirect; yet these two in combination give rise to an endless series of maneuvers.

Almost everything that you do will be to advance your argument or defend it, which in most legal battles means that you are also trying to weaken your opponent's arguments. It is key to note that you must also do what you can to make the jury like you and/or your client i.e., for the jury members to want to rule in you favor or for your client. It is far easier to convince someone to agree with you when they *want* to. Although you will be in fight mode during the trial, it is great if you can offer some levity or humor when the chance arises. During jury selection is often the best time to try to show some humanity and humor to get the jury comfortable with you. Many jurors will not completely understand what you or a key witness is saying, especially when expert witness testimony is involved, so it is an unfortunate reality that a juror may subconsciously or directly simply side with the lawyer and client they like better. Talking about your spouse and kids in jury selection can humanize you with the jury. You may think you are starting at level zero when you meet them, but you are not. They will blame you for having to be there and they may immediately classify you as scum simply because you are a lawyer. You must presume you are starting in negative-like territory from the first moment and you need to get out of that zone very fast. I often talk about my wife who is a special-needs teacher. I also use self-depreciating humor such as, a short person I may note when it is my turn to talk to the prospective jurors in jury selection that, although the state or court introduced me, I will reintroduce myself saying I am pretty short so now that I am closer, do any of you recognize me from any past occurrence, as part of the conflicts pocket, etc. Starting with a joke can do a great deal to help dig yourself out of the hole you start in simply by being a lawyer to begin with.

11. The direct and the indirect lead on to each other in turn. It is like moving in a circle—you never come to an end. Who can exhaust the possibilities of their combination?

Your witnesses offer evidence, but they also seek to discredit evidence from the other side. A popular way to bolster what your witness has said, when it is in direct contradiction to what one of their witnesses said, is to poke holes in the credibility of the other side's expert or key witness. Similarly, it's important to discredit their witnesses with a better explanation of an event by your more able and likeable witness. You will also need to highlight a seemingly benign point from an expert or other witness when needed, so it stays with the jury. You have to raise a very important point early on when you can really explain to the jury why it is key, though you will need to do it again in closing arguments. Classic voice inflections and pauses are effective, but in modern times, if it is a key point, you need to deliver it with a visual aid if at all possible.

12. The onset of troops is like the rush of a torrent which will even roll stones along in its course.

You must always choose your steps wisely at trial. Even though a decision may have to be made on the fly, you have to keep in mind how one decision may lock you in to a certain path during the rest of the case and may rule out other possible avenues or arguments. It is best before trial to do everything you or your team can do to go over the possibilities, so you are ready with a pre-determined plan of action for a particular occurrence. You can't very well claim an alibi and then later argue to a jury the defendant was there, but he didn't do it based on self-defense, etc. You can't claim very easily that the opponent eyewitness couldn't see very well due to poor lighting but that your eyewitness who was close by could.

13. The quality of decision is like the well-timed swoop of a falcon which enables it to strike and destroy its victim.

A person is granted a certain amount of leeway to shoot from the hip or make split-second critical decisions. A falconer does not simple acquire a bird and then through some sort of force or ability make it perform a maneuver just the way they want on the first try. Practice and experience make the falconer and falcon a good team. So too it is with trial skills. Preparing to the point where you can respond to an objection with a Zen-like natural flow, i.e., with no need for extra thinking, will make you as fast as possible. Practice and planning for what you can try to predict is what will make it seem like your action at trial is effortless or based on natural instinct of a hunting bird acquiring a meal.

You also need to practice with your team. If you have a new member on your team or an individual who doesn't have much courtroom experience, they need to be open to mock trial segments with you, so you and your teammates can be better in-tune before trial.

14. Thus the momentum of one skilled in war is overwhelming and his attack precisely regulated.

The ability to make war in the arena of the law will not come to you in an instant. You must work to develop your skills over the years. Of course, you must fight on a given day with the ability and knowledge you have acquired up until that point. You can't make yourself have more experience, but you can always be the better-prepared lawyer. This is not the first time or the last time this will be pointed out in this book for good reason.

15. Energy may be likened to the bending of a crossbow; decision, to the releasing of a trigger.

Timing is everything. Only through practice and experience do you get a feeling of when to let go of the bow string and how far to pull it back to make sure that you hit your target. With time and practice you can instinctively know how to place your hands on the bow and arrow, to feel the amount of strength you need, calculate distance to target, factor in wind and other variables, know when to let go, all in a second or less, while the war is raging all around you. With experience you will be shocked at how quickly you can calculate in a trial when you have done what is needed to prepare to the utmost.

16. Amid the turmoil and tumult of battle, there may be seeming disorder and yet no real disorder at all; amid confusion and chaos, your array may be without head or tail, yet it will be proof against defeat.

Sometimes a trial can seem unpredictable and therefore impossible to plan for in every way. Witnesses may change their story because they are nervous or lying. Evidence may have gone missing. The order of witnesses may change, etc. Experience will teach you to get used to surprises. Most of the time the slam-dunk trials settle one way or the other. Trials that occur are often close calls to begin with and a change in what was expected can seem jarring. Keep in mind that it will happen during every trial you have and that it will also happen to your opponent. Although preparation is the cornerstone of a well-litigated trial, your ability to handle a surprise will be key. The greatest generals over time had to deal with a great deal of surprises. You can't have a battle with thousands of soldiers and presume everything will go according to plan. Even in a relatively short trial with half a dozen witnesses, things can and will still go wrong or at least differently from what you expected. Keep in mind that the jury does not know your plan and they may only know by the look on your face and how you react that you are not happy about something that happened. When dealing with a twist or turn it is wise to keep your cool and not show frustration to the jury. Jury members should always think things are going just as you thought they were to. Many jurors don't fully understand what is happening, but they can see if you are angry or out of sorts.

In one of my first DUI cases as a prosecutor, when I finally got the job I wanted in the best paying office, I had a plain-vanilla case with an officer who had been on the force for twenty years. I hadn't asked him how many DUI cases he had handled, as he seemed to know the material well and he covered them well in the trial. In trial I asked him how many DUIs he had done while serving the community as an officer for almost two decades, and he said "well this is the third in my career." I was shocked but I had to remember not to show it, so I quickly pivoted to noting that since it was such a rare case for him as a senior administrator who is not in the field often, that he must remember this case very well. Not my proudest moment, but when we won, and when I polled the jury, they were a very talkative bunch, and nobody said anything about it.

17. Apparent confusion is a product of good order; apparent cowardice, of courage; apparent weakness of strength.

Through great efforts you can look out of sorts when you want to, even though you are very prepared. There can certainly be reasons for seeming that way to your opponent but not the jury.

18. Hiding order beneath the cloak of disorder is simply a question of subdivision; concealing courage under a show of timidity presupposes a fund of latent energy; masking strength with weakness is to be affected by tactical dispositions.

There is never a need to boast. Foolish attorneys will brag about how ready they are or how strong their case is just before trial. By this point the opponent should know the strength of the case or lack thereof. They should know if they should settle or not. Although you may point out strengths to try to get a last-minute offer (if your client wants that), there is no need to take it too far. It is one thing to say my case is strong, but never say *I* will beat *you*. Don't make it personal. A busy prosecutor who simply hates you may consciously or unconsciously rearrange their trial priorities if double-booked, which is often the case in busier jurisdictions. Attorneys that are deemed to be 'assholes' will never get a better deal and will always find their way to the top of the state's list of priority cases to fight all the way. You may like having more fun trials to fight but that is not in the best interest of your clients.

19. Thus one who is skillful at keeping the enemy on the move maintains deceitful appearances, according to which the enemy will act. He sacrifices something, that the enemy may snatch at it.

Within the bounds of ethics rules, you can feign weakness when you have strength with the other side. It is a delicate balance, and just like in war you want the other side to think you are so strong they should cut their losses, especially when you are not. However, there is often a point of no return in a case when you know a deal is not likely. For example, on a criminal case when you know the state won't offer a deal worth taking, there is no reason to boast about the case and make the state think they should spend more time preparing their case. Let them think your client just wants a trial and you don't feel good about your chances, etc., and they may spend more time on other cases and not making sure everything is ready for your trial with them. Never underestimate the laziness of the other side and encourage it. You should not slow your pace because you think they may be unprepared, but you can certainly attempt to make them feel so confident that they need not bother and can ride out the case on cruise control. This can be contrary to earlier positions of this text, but it must be kept in mind to be used at the correct time in your practice. As is the case with most rules, there are exceptions.

This rule not only applies to a grand strategic point of view but also to a tactical level as well. You may well still tout the strength of your case until the last minute to get a deal while feigning ignorance of a case on point or hinting at a weak witness to draw attention away from those points or try to get the other side to focus on a particular witness that you think will be key to your case when you know it is not. This may lead the other side to spend their limited time or too much time on a red herring.

20. By holding out baits, he keeps him on the march; then with a body of picked men he lies in wait for him.

Our system has a code of ethics and at the same time it is an adversarial system. Supplying discovery in mass for example is a long-employed tactic. To bury a key piece of evidence that hurts you, in the midst of a massive discovery dump of dozens of banker boxes is a typical example. To keep an opponent pouring over worthless material and wasting time is obviously a wonderful thing, if possible. Even at the tactical level during trial you may say that a certain witness is going to blow the doors off the other side's case tomorrow and let them spend valuable time that evening trying to figure out why, when in reality they have nothing particularly significant to offer beyond what was already disclosed.

21. The clever combatant looks to the effect of combined energy and does not require too much from individuals. Hence his ability to pick out the right men and utilize combined energy.

A trial team must wisely handle the task assignments. Every team member must know the relative importance of each task assigned to them. Also, a trial team leader must, of course, choose the right people for the most important tasks that they can't do themselves. The leader taking on too much of the work can lead to defeat.

22. When he utilizes combined energy, his fighting men become, as it were, like unto rolling logs or stones. For it is the nature of a log or stone to remain motionless on level ground, and to move when on a slope; if four-cornered, to come to a standstill, but if round-shaped, to go rolling down.

By getting the right team member tackling the right task, he or she will be able to get things on a roll toward the necessary objective. If their skill set fits the task assigned by you, then they will produce results in line with the energy spent. If you assign your team poorly, precious time and resources will be wasted.

23. Thus the energy developed by good fighting men is as the momentum of a round stone rolled down a mountain thousands of feet in height. So much on the subject of energy.

Knowing your team from past experience with a given team member is the best way to know how to employ them in current cases. When you have new people on the team, you should do what you can via socializing, etc. to see what they seem capable of. You should check with past references and have honest conversations with them about assignments and their abilities. To accidentally set them up for failure is also to set yourself up for failure.

VI. Weak Points and Strong

1. Sun Tzu said: Whoever is first in the field and awaits the coming of the enemy, will be fresh for the fight; whoever is second in the field and has to hasten to battle will arrive exhausted.

It is far better to get an enemy to try to comport to your strategy then to try to scramble to handle their chosen plan. This is not easy but can lead to great results in a case or trial. If there is a key witness that you need to talk to, don't wait for the deposition; if at all possible, send a private investigator or employ some other method to get helpful facts locked in from the start. Facts have a way of changing if you don't lock them in. Although you have to react to moves your opponent may be appearing to make, you still need to keep your plans on track and see if you can get them to line up with the facts.

In the context of a simple DUI trial, the prosecutor, on a low breath test case, may simply decide that they won't even bother bringing in the breath test expert and may choose to only go to trial on the failure of field tests and the erratic driving behavior. A defense lawyer who is basing their case on the test being well within the margin of error, may be in trouble if the expert is not subpoenaed to the trial as they have been forced into a strategy not of their choosing. If a person looks bad on the field tests but only tested 2/1000ths above the limit, then that may have been the best argument.

2. Therefore, the clever combatant imposes his will on the enemy, but does not allow the enemy's will to be imposed on him.

Achieving this advantageous position is hard and is often tailored to each specific case. For example, getting a prosecutor to focus their witness on discrediting your theory can often lead to them neglecting the elements they must prove. This can allow you an opportunity to find reasonable doubt through your argument or an unexpected opening that comes from their neglect.

3. By holding out advantages to him, he can cause the enemy to approach of his own accord; or, by inflicting damage, he can make it impossible for the enemy to draw near.

In an adversarial system you can often find something to draw out your opponent. Whether in trial or just talking to a lawyer earlier in the case you can dangle a false angle. Such as a prosecutor saying your officer witness in a criminal case is not very experienced when in fact they have testified before and did well. You can plant a seed in the head of an opponent to fixate on an easy target when it is not truly a weak point at all. You can also draw out an opponent in simple conversation about the case in the hopes they give you a clue etc. that they normally wouldn't. You lose nothing by trying to get the opponent talking, of course. Trial lawyers by nature are not introverted or subtle people. You may be surprised at how many talk to you about key information even on the morning of trial in a last ditch effort to impress upon you to get a last-minute settlement out of you so they can go tend to the pile of work from other cases on their desk.

4. If the enemy is taking his ease, he can harass him; if well supplied with food, he can starve him out; if quietly encamped, he can force him to move.

Take advantage of your advantages. Most private defense lawyers can spend more time on a criminal case then a prosecutor can. A personal injury lawyer with a handful of good cases will have more time than an insurance lawyer who has to defend numerous claims against the company and also may be a salaried lawyer with no significant bonus system in place. If you are affluent, then spend more on expert witnesses. If you are experienced, be sure to plan to object to things a new attorney may not know how to respond to, and don't presume that they know all that you do on procedural rules, etc. If the other lawyer has a temper, then try to bait him in front of a jury to make him seem more disagreeable to them.

5. Appear at points which the enemy must hasten to defend; march swiftly to places where you are not expected.

Although the legal process requires disclosure and discovery, you can still shine light on less important areas and keep more important or flawed areas in the shadows so your opponent can't see them clearly. You should also try to feign toward topics or areas of the case in front of the opponent to get them to direct their attention there when you think it will not amount to any gains. Let them focus more on your stronger witnesses and not spend as much of their time preparing to break down your weaker ones. It costs nothing for you to talk up a concern you have with one of your stronger witnesses when really you think they will be fine when the time comes. Your opponent may think they are vulnerable and spend precious time trying to find a flaw when there isn't one. Mentioning your expert seems to be getting on in years and may retire soon may subtly draw your opponent to them when really, they are just as good as they always have been.

Conversely, you will want to attack weak points that your opponent may not see as weak. You may uncover an impeachment topic in a deposition and your opponent does not clearly see it. Hours and hours of depositions can lead to any lawyer getting distracted or tired and not at their best. There may be a weak point that you highlight with great fanfare at a deposition to try to get your opponent to yield without trial but there also may be points you don't want to draw attention to and subtlety lock in, so that you can swiftly attack the weak point at trial where hopefully the opponent is not ready to defend it properly. Such decisions are unique to your situations and only you can decide the best choice in any given case.

6. An army may march great distances without distress, if it marches through country where the enemy is not.

Location, location, location. You can always set depositions in your office or city and make the other side travel. Don't underestimate the financial costs of travel as well, especially for a smaller law firm opponent. Your witness will feel safer and protected in your office, especially a victim or other lay witness. The better and more comfortable they feel in a very uncomfortable situation will keep them at their best. We often can forget that while we enjoy and look forward to the fight, our client or other key witnesses may be dreading it. They may be losing sleep the night before a deposition or having other complications from their anxiety. Even general lay witnesses who are not a client or plaintiff may yet be terrified about going to court and could come across as unreliable based solely on their nerves. Anything you can do to make them more comfortable is worth it. Even great athletes can have an off day and often those occur as they are out of sorts for some reason. When you can make it easier for your people you should, even if it is harder for you.

7. You can be sure of succeeding in your attacks if you only attack places which are undefended. You can ensure the safety of your defense if you only hold positions that cannot be attacked.

There is no such thing as a witness that can't be compromised or an exhibit that can't be discredited. However, you must do what you can to keep key elements of your case protected. Conversely you can and must pick places that are assailable and worthy of your time and resources when trying to stop an opponent from proving their case. Every case is different but seeing these points in each case is critical. Scoring a win on a witness that doesn't affect the outcome will be worthless. Witnesses and exhibits must be measured on their value. Their value is to be calculated based on how they boost your argument that your elements were shown to the jury or your argument that the opponent has not met their burden to show a necessary element. In our battlefield, that is how you get a win. If you keep attacking a strong opposition witness with no success it will serve to enhance them with the jury. If you can only get a little bit out of them, then get it and get out. There is no need to keep hitting them only to have them deflect the shots and get more successful face time with the jury.

Defense attorneys rarely represent an innocent client; the only way to win is to make it so your opponent can't show what they need to show to meet their elements criteria from the jury instructions. When preparing for a jury trial, the jury instructions are the place to start. Without knowing what you or your opponent *need* to say in closing, you can't properly prepare for any other part of the trial or even measure a plea offer.

8. Hence that general is skillful in attack whose opponent does not know what to defend; and he is skillful in defense whose opponent does not know what to attack.

Unlike war, we give opening statements in trial that predict what will be seen and heard and why it will be important. Although openings are not to be used for argument, we of course will try to insert subtle arguments (and sometimes not so subtle ones) when possible. The jury needs to know what will happen for numerous reasons as you can't count on them noticing a key point on the fourth day of a trial, for example. You do not need to tip your opponent to a key strike that you plan for a witness or other matter. A strategy can be seen from your opening, and in most cases the opponent will have a general idea of what you plan to do. You must start getting the jury on your side in opening, especially if you are on the defense, as they may not hear from you as much as you would want for some time. It is key to get your client's side out there, so it stays in the jury's mind. You can still hand some surprises to your opponent to learn of the hard way AND still bring attention to key points during the trial with voice inflection, pauses, etc. to help make those moments stick with the jury. You may have spent years working on a case and have known that a key fact or witness is paramount to the case. However, a jury of disinterested and perhaps poorly educated people with no dog in the fight, may not see what you hope will be obvious to them, without you taking great measures in directing and guiding them.

9. O divine art of subtlety and secrecy! Through you we learn to be invisible, through you inaudible; and hence we can hold the enemy's fate in our hands.

You can follow every ethics rule and still leave surprises for your opponent. It is an adversarial system and if, through discovery, certain key factors never occur to them, that is not your fault. The order or method of production can help hide key facts as well. A discovery dump or producing one key fact in a different batch of materials than a relating key fact can be helpful and cost you nothing. You must divulge some positive material in order to secure a favorable offer, but for the material you do keep in reserve for trial you must do what you can to keep it a secret until you spring the trap or launch an unexpected attack. Your ability to not tip your cap through a long and adversarial process can be key to success. Fighting the temptation to brag about or bring undue attention to material that you plan to use to great affect is hard over a long litigation fight. Highlighting some facts to get a positive resolution while holding other points back is the tightrope walk of litigation. Just as in battle, you can lose a battle before one shot has even been fired.

10. You may advance and be absolutely irresistible, if you make for the enemy's weak points; you may retire and be safe from pursuit if your movements are more rapid than those of the enemy.

There will be opportunities to get your opponent focused on what you want them to, just as you may want the jury to be following key points. If you can get your opponent to focus on what you want them to (because you think your point will hold up) then you are using up the opponent's resources on a fruitless mission. For example, if credibility of a witness is key, and under cross she holds up well, then that can score a great deal of points with the jury, both for the witness credibility and the opposition appearing to be unlikable or untrustworthy.

Often lawyers will leave a great answer hanging in the air and wait to go to the next question, which is good, but if you have what you need, then move on to the next topic. If you have accomplished the mission of the pocket of questions, then don't try to get too much gravy, as it can lead to the opponent catching up or rebounding. Also, scoring a quick point on cross that is not successfully rebutted during evidence can leave a strong point for closing that your opponent can't do much to go back and remedy.

11. If we wish to fight, the enemy can be forced to an engagement even though he be sheltered behind a high rampart and a deep ditch. All we need do is attack some other place that he will be obliged to relieve.

If the opponent is holding strong on a point or making a solid attack of you, then you can try to bait them into a new focus area. The longer they pound a weak point of yours, the more likely it is that it sticks with the jury. If you can bait them, do so. In the heat of the moment, emotions can best draw someone out from a safe place toward making a bad decision.

12. If we do not wish to fight, we can prevent the enemy from engaging us even though the lines of our encampment be merely traced out on the ground. All we need do is to throw something odd and unaccountable in his way.

The jury doesn't know what we planned to happen, and sometimes the only way jurors know it is not going exactly as we wanted is because of our face and reactions. Showing emotions on our face or frantically scribbling a note on a legal pad to show another team member will be a clear sign to a juror that something is amiss. We must remember that things won't always go the way we thought they would. When something does go wrong, it can still be a shock to us or our opponent. If you distract your opponent or throw them off just a bit, then it can have serious impacts on their case progression or witness comfort. A timely objection with an offer of proof or a request for a recess can throw off your opponent right at a key point.

13. By discovering the enemy's dispositions and remaining invisible ourselves, we can keep our forces concentrated, while the enemy's must be divided.

We have to look for hints and tips as to what the opponent is going to target. Sometimes it can be obvious ahead of trial, and sometimes you won't get a clear idea until you are underway and then something occurs to you. One of the best appellate arguments points I ever thought of happened to me in the restroom on the morning of oral argument. There is no reason to broadcast what you think are your best or critical points. On many occasions, before trial, you will want to talk up the strengths of your case to get a better plea offer, but you don't have to show them your ace cards either. It is a delicate balance that is often only clearly delineated on a case-by-case basis. To distract your opponent, you may want to even offer up something as important as a red herring, without making it seem like you don't fully understand your case.

14. We can form a single united body, while the enemy must split up into fractions. Hence there will be a whole pitted against separate parts of a whole, which means that we shall be many to the enemy's few.

Arguably the most important resource a lawyer has is time. If you can get your opponent to waste time on an issue that does not truly matter in the end or to prepare for a possible argument that you don't end up employing, then you have successfully kept them from working on material that does matter.

When dealing with your case, you must keep your team together. While they do tasks that you can't micromanage, you do want to use the current technology and everything at your disposal to stay on the same page with one another and when you can, with the client as well.

15. And if we are able thus to attack an inferior force with a superior one, our opponents will be in dire straits.

As in war, if you can keep their soldiers from the key locations of the battlefield then you improve your chances to win that location or key point. That point or high ground, if you will, may be key to controlling a large portion of, or even the whole case. Their time to prepare is often analogous to the troops they can put in the field. Looking at a case and knowing from where the battles are coming, you must analyze the advantages or disadvantages that are built into the case. You may be able to look at the elements of the case and see how you will prove them, but you also should consider how competent the witnesses are who will fight the specific battles with you. Bringing a good point to the jury may only be effective if the witness who bears it is credible and delivers it strongly. A stronger expert witness then the opponent may be the key to success even if the facts can't be altered or enhanced. A stronger witness armed with the same tools as another will increase your chances to win.

16. The spot where we intend to fight must not be made known; for then the enemy will have to prepare against a possible attack at several different points; and his forces being thus distributed in many directions, the numbers we shall have to face at any given point will be proportionately few.

In complex litigation this can be easier, but even in a simple case like a DUI it can still be done. Say, for example, you have a low-test DUI that is right at or below the margin of error and close to the legal limit. Obviously, the other side will know that you must attack the validity of that test result. You don't have to indicate, until the last moment, how you do it. If the defendant had an open container you may choose to argue that the test was higher than his breath alcohol was when driving as the beer was still being absorbed. You may focus on the testing procedures being in error. You may choose to target the calibration of the breath test device. You may focus on performance of the FSTs to show the test must be wrong and the defendant was not impaired, etc. Of course, you want to let the state wonder which angle you will focus on, in the hopes they don't put as much time into the one you plan to rely most heavily on. Let them prepare witnesses and demonstrative aids or exhibits that become next to worthless based on your argument. Let them end up not admitting all their previously marked exhibits, so the jury, in deliberations, wonders why the state's exhibits skip numbers, etc.

17. For should the enemy strengthen his van, he will weaken his rear; should he strengthen his rear, he will weaken his van;

should he strengthen his left, he will weaken his right; should he strengthen his right, he will weaken his left. If he sends reinforcements everywhere, he will everywhere be weak.

Let them figure out how to draw up their closing PowerPoint or how much witness prep time to spend with the witnesses on each possible issue, etc. They will waste at least some time preparing for an attack that you won't be spending any time on preparing. Maybe they will have a PowerPoint slide that is not needed any longer and they fumble past it during their closing argument.

18. Numerical weakness comes from having to prepare against possible attacks; numerical strength, from compelling our adversary to make these preparations against us.

Your opposition will want to and should prepare their witnesses and exhibits in anticipation of meeting the elements but also in dealing with your various possible arguments regarding the elements of the charge or suit. Technology is wonderful but it takes time to prepare PowerPoints and video snippets to use in closing, etc. If they are not sure which points you will target, you can really affect the quality of tools they will have prepared to use in closing or with key witnesses. Also, they will likely want to prepare an opening that addresses some of your possible positions, but they may not, out of fear to muddy the waters or look like they were promising something that never comes. They will have to spend time on issues that will be moot. They will want to prepare a closing and will be challenged by not knowing exactly how to direct it.

19. Knowing the place and the time of the coming battle, we may concentrate from the greatest distances in order to fight.

We have to determine the key points of attack we want to focus on as well. As in battle, such determinations vary from case to case and battlefield to battlefield. Of course, being able to see the high ground or other advantageous position in each situation will be key to winning the fight. If you put the work in you should be able to see the fighting issues and their pros and cons well ahead of trial.

20. But if neither time nor place be known, then the left wing will be impotent to succor the right, the right equally impotent to succor the left, the van unable to relieve the rear, or the rear to support the van. How much more so if the furthest portions of the army are anything under a hundred LI apart, and even the nearest are separated by several LI!

You need to keep in mind that each battle or key fact for an element is all part of the big picture: the guilty or not-guilty verdict for the plaintiff or defense. Keep an eye on the big picture and don't get too focused on the trees that make up the forest. In law it is not just the trees that make the forest, but you have to focus on how many trees will it take to make the jury of twelve possibly very different people see a group of trees as the same forest, so to speak.

21. Though according to my estimate the soldiers of Yueh exceed our own in number, that shall advantage them nothing in the matter of victory. I say then that victory can be achieved.

Small firms win suits against large firms. Guilty defendants are acquitted in spite of talented prosecutors. This is because of the variables involved and discussed throughout this book.

22. Though the enemy be stronger in numbers, we may prevent him from fighting. Scheme so as to discover his plans and the likelihood of their success.

You must do what you can in depositions and even in trial to determine what the opponent seeks to do and what they will target. You won't ever have the proverbial crystal ball. You can never be sure, but making good estimations and predictions is a key part of the art of litigation.

23. Rouse him, and learn the principle of his activity or inactivity. Force him to reveal himself, so as to find out his vulnerable spots.

The system tries to have rules that make it so you know what an opponent will argue. A criminal defendant, for example, often has to give notifications of certain defenses in many jurisdictions. Although some will hesitate to give too much away in depositions, it can be worth it to get a witness locked in while under oath. A deposition is often the best chance you have to get a clear indicator of what a witness has to offer and in combination with other information you can have a much clearer view of what the other side has as a whole. Even if you have to show your cards a bit, it will be worth it to see theirs so you can be ready for trial most of the time. In one case you may want to show a lot of your cards while in another you will be wisely hesitant to show any of your best points early on. The right way to proceed on any given case should be determined on the particulars of that case and the variables in play as covered in this book.

24. Carefully compare the opposing army with your own, so that you may know where strength is superabundant and where it is deficient.

It is easy to say that you can have a surprise in store for trial, but many cases will be pending for months if not years, and it is hard to expect that as something you can count on. It is wiser to explore what you will see at trial as much as possible, even if you must show what you have, to a degree.

25. In making tactical dispositions, the highest pitch you can attain is to conceal them; conceal your dispositions, and you will be safe from the prying of the subtlest spies, from the machinations of the wisest brains.

The discovery process does not mean you have to divulge strategy or even highlight key facts. You must do what you can to aim more light on those items that may attract attention without damage and keep key matters in the shadows, so they are less prevalent. While you may choose to highlight strong points to motivate plea offers, you must downplay and pick at possible week points with the same objective in mind.

26. How victory may be produced for them out of the enemy's own tactics—that is what the multitude cannot comprehend.

Achieving a win due to an opponent's mistake or miscalculation is the pinnacle of skill for a lawyer. You can never plan for your opponent to stumble. You have to prepare your case as best as you can, assuming they will make no mistakes. You can't be so locked into your plans as to not be able to adapt to mistakes as you see them. You will also notice flaws in their plans as you proceed and will need to decide whether to adjust your plans accordingly. You have to strike a balance between not wanting to jump on a mistake for the sake of 'catching' your opponent and deciding as you go if it will increase your chances more to do so or just stay on your planned path. The north star for any case is the model jury instructions that most courts have. In the end those should determine who wins the case, and you can't lose sight of them while making an adjustment to take advantage of a flaw in the enemy's plan.

27. All men can see the tactics whereby I conquer, but what none can see is the strategy out of which victory is evolved.

It is one thing to see how an opponent prevailed in a trial after the fact. Hindsight is always 20/20. The skill you must acquire is to see how to win while the matter is pending and hopefully before the opponent, so they cannot effectively counter. It is the nature of litigation that through depositions and discovery your opponent will at least see some of your plan ahead of trial. You will need to operate in such a way that they may see your strength but not know exactly what you plan to do. As has already been noted in this text, this is a delicate balance that you will need to achieve. You will even want your opponent to know how strong your case is to get a settlement, yet you can't tip them to everything that you have or can do, as when no deal is reached, they will know too much about your plans and counter them. This is an easy thing to read here but not at all easy to do. Finding how much you can give without giving up too much is a fine line and one that will move drastically for each case. The unique factors that will indicate where the line is are impossible to generalize and can only be seen or felt by those engaged in the case.

28. Do not repeat the tactics which have gained you one victory, but let your methods be regulated by the infinite variety of circumstances.

Trials are as different as battlefields. The ground you fight on will often be very different, as are conditions in a battle. Also, in law technology changes, the law changes and new variables will appear that were not present a handful of years earlier. Although experience is invaluable, as it helps you see what you need to see, the complexities of each unique case will make it necessary to find new ways to win. Even in similar types of cases, over the years there may be some steps you can recycle and things a new opponent has not seen you do, but the scene of a crime, or motive or number of witnesses, etc. will always change. A car accident case will still have variables in its occurrence and in the medical rehabilitation process, etc. You don't need to completely reinvent the wheel for every trial, especially with new opponents. You can use what has worked in the past and tailer it to the specific needs and specific circumstances of the present case.

29. Military tactics are like unto water; for water in its natural course runs away from high places and hastens downwards.

Although the variables are different, it can be said that the nature of fighting is similar from case to case and arena to arena. In law the high ground is still the high ground whether one or one thousand soldiers hold it. A cornered opponent will still fight as if trapped. The nature and flow of every trial will have some similarities. You will always want the jury to like you; you must always be as prepared as possible; you must always take whatever natural advantages are given to you, like a sympathetic witness, etc.

30. So in war, the way is to avoid what is strong and to strike at what is weak.

Your opponents will always have a weakness to their case, or you wouldn't be in trial. Even if you are going to trial because you have nothing to lose and no offer worth taking, there will be some aspect of the other side's case that can be exploited. The key is to find it and to be sure that what you see is what the jury will see. You have to foresee what the jury will consider to be the weakness of your opponent's case, the flaw that resonates with them. Whether it should be the issue or not, you must see what they see as critical.

31. Water shapes its course according to the nature of the ground over which it flows; the soldier works out his victory in relation to the foe whom he is facing.

The ground you are on in trial is not just the lay of the land of the court room and the proclivities of the judge. It is not just the facts and law for the jurisdiction. It is also the makeup of the jury. You won't know what they will be like exactly until days or hours before trial at best. All of them have differing opinions and viewpoints, often based on the vantage point of a person with no legal experience. The flow of the water will go as they see it, so you must see it as they do.

32. Therefore, just as water retains no constant shape, so in warfare there are no constant conditions.

You must read the jury as the case unfolds before them. Facial expressions, head nods, and other subtle clues may (and often should) send you on a different path with a key witness or argument. Knowing people will be as important for the lawyer as knowing the capabilities of a weapon is for the soldier. You can look to see what you can find on them on social media but for the most part you have to use your gut based on what you see and on stereotypes which may or may not fit in with your politically correct view of the world.

33. He who can modify his tactics in relation to his opponent and thereby succeed in winning, may be called a heaven-born captain.

As much as you will prepare for a trial you must also be ready to change course as needed once it commences. Plan B can very quickly move ahead of plan A based on unseen variables or your gut feeling toward the jury. Such choices when prison for life or millions of dollars are at stake, should not be taken lightly, but you must be able to move and not let fear paralyze you in a dying plan. The client may be the one to make the call, and when you approach them with your concerns you must still appear very much in control and confident and not alarm them too much if you want to change things. Of course, telling them ahead of time that changes and adjustments are often made during the trial will be key to managing their expectations.

34. The five elements (water, fire, wood, metal, earth) are not always equally predominant; the four seasons make way for each other in turn. There are short days and long; the moon has its periods of waning and waxing.

Society changes. The makeup of a jury is very different now than thirty years ago. Jurors expect to see visual aids and CSI-type evidence in every criminal case, even a low-level offence. They may be more conservative or more liberal than they once were on issues. More conservative or even racist jurors will be more open about their thoughts in deliberation. Liberal jurors may be more aggressive than they once were, in order to be heard or listened to by the other jurors. Society is less shocked by crime scenes, yet more offended by inappropriate harassment, etc. due to changes in societal norms. What may have seen like a clever quip by a lawyer with a witness before may make the lawyer just seem like an asshole today. It is close to impossible to win a trial where the jury does not like you.

VII. Maneuvering

1. Sun Tzu said: In war, the general receives his commands from the sovereign.

The client controls the case, and it is rightly said to be *their* case. They determine what a good deal is or a win, as it were. Of all the opinions of people involved, be they the judge, the expert witness, the jury, etc., the client's opinion means the most, and you are duty bound to give it the attention it deserves.

2. Having collected an army and concentrated his forces, he must blend and harmonize the different elements thereof before pitching his camp.

In addition to juggling the witnesses, possible arguments, possible backup arguments, the judge's pre-trial rulings, the client's thoughts and everything else, you must try to get them all on the same page and keep them there.

3. After that comes tactical maneuvering, of which there is nothing more difficult. The difficulty of tactical maneuvering consists in turning the devious into the direct, and misfortune into gain.

You will need to decide when to disclose discovery material, when to do depositions, and highlighting strong points without exposing your plans to the opposition. You also have to keep your whole team on board with any sudden change in direction. Communication within the team is critical.

4. Thus, to take a long and circuitous route, after enticing the enemy out of the way, and though starting after him, to contrive to reach the goal before him, shows knowledge of the artifice of deviation.

If you can outspend or outwork your opponent, then do so. In many cases you may not have more resources than they do, but when you do, you should. If you don't, then you must be sure to not be baited into a detour to nowhere. To boost your chances, employ the best experts and investigators you can. Although you may be motivated by billable hours to expand on everything you can, you must also keep in mind then when it comes to trial, the jury will have limited interest and limited intelligence to process everything you want them to. You must simplify matters as much as possible for them and keep it straightforward enough for them to not misunderstand your points. You have to keep in mind that you have spent so much time on your case by the time it gets to trial, and they have spent none.

5. Maneuvering with an army is advantageous; with an undisciplined multitude, most dangerous.

You have to keep all of your lawyers and staff as well as your client and your witnesses on the same page. There may even be ethics rules that prevent you from telling a witness something that another has shared, yet you must keep them all on the same path and at the right pace. Not every member of your team will be as disciplined as you would want them to be. Expert witnesses are often vain and don't want to take input from a lowly attorney. Witnesses may get emotional or under stress say something they are not supposed to or forget to say something they are supposed to. Your fellow lawyers may err, and it could be up to you to remedy the issue and stay on the path. Do remember and tell everyone, especially the client, that there will be surprises. Even the most prepared lawyer will encounter some sort of event that requires alteration to plans before and during trial. It is the nature of how things move, and all involved must be ready for change in unison.

6. If you set a fully equipped army in march in order to snatch an advantage, the chances are that you will be too late. On the other hand, to detach a flying column for the purpose involves the sacrifice of its baggage and stores.

Every part of your team must have a leader or conductor. They can't possibly know what every other member is doing and thinking, so it is up to the lead attorney to coordinate things in such a way that the others know what they are to do and what others are to take care of and when. It is a great challenge but if ignored it can lead to great confusion which could lead to a waste of precious time or a display of confusion in front of the jury that diminishes the jurors' confidence in your side.

7. Thus, if you order your men to roll up their buff-coats, and make forced marches without halting day or night, covering double the usual distance at a stretch, doing a hundred LI in order to wrest an advantage, the leaders of all your three divisions will fall into the hands of the enemy.

If your lieutenants are too aggressive and don't stay in lock step with the overall plan, they can run into issues where they expose too much of your plan to the enemy or make some other blunder. Without micromanaging them or restricting their capabilities, you have to keep them on the general path that has been chosen. This can occur in trial preparation phases or in the trial itself, be they out of your sight for a presumed minor deposition or making an error with an opponent witness on the stand.

8. The stronger men will be in front, the jaded ones will fall behind, and on this plan only one-tenth of your army will reach its destination.

Keeping complex litigation on the same path is always a challenge. You have to give tasks to your team with the knowledge that your better people must have the harder tasks, so they don't outpace the less capable. You must also not overburden yourself when deciding what to delegate and what to keep. If you are the strongest on your team, and you take on key tasks, then you must not overextend yourself as well. Keep in mind that many generals and leaders are not the best tactical fighters and can be successful as great managers of officers. Most generals in a one-on-one fight with a young soldier can lose. They may have experience on their side, but the soldier may be younger and stronger or more familiar with a martial art that determines the winner. A great boxer, for example, may lose to an MMA fighter if there are no rule-setting boundaries, even if they are the best boxer in the world. A good team leader does not let ego block their view of the case and they may realize that a younger member should be the one to handle a key cross or closing.

9. If you march fifty LI in order to outmaneuver the enemy, you will lose the leader of your first division, and only half your force will reach the goal.

Of course, there can be strength in numbers. If your team is not on the same page, it can cause them a great deal of precious time to get back on the same page. During pre-trial or trial, the focus must be in unison, or your army can't bring its strength to the point of attack.

10. If you march thirty LI with the same object, two-thirds of your army will arrive.

We live in amazing technologically advanced times. The concept of emails, FaceTime, and other leaps in communication technology have changed the game. A lawyer and their co-counselor or expert witness can speak live about a case from the other side of the world. The ability to stay on the same page with your team has never been easier, provided that you prioritize it as necessary to the success of the case.

11. We may take it then that an army without its baggage-train is lost; without provisions it is lost; without bases of supply it is lost.

I have never gone to trial with just technology. Called me old-fashioned but although I do lean heavily on technology, I still bring a physical trial notebook with me. That could be my age or paranoia, but of course we must be prepared for critical moments like depositions, motion hearings, and trial for our technology to fail. What if your PowerPoint doesn't work for your closing? What if video footage of a crime scene won't play? You can't know when such a thing may occur, so you must be ready for any aid to be unavailable. Depending on the judge, you may be able to get a continuance if, for example, your expert is delayed due to weather. However, most judges will not allow a postponement of a closing to the following day based on tech issues.

12. We cannot enter into alliances until we are acquainted with the designs of our neighbors.

An entire book could be written on the perils of what to say or not say to other lawyers in a large multi-plaintiff or multi-defendant tort action, or with a codefendant in a criminal case. It is important to note here that maneuvering within your own team may be a challenge, so trying to coordinate with another party's team, even when you think you can trust them, is obviously an even greater challenge and still one that can lead to disaster for both.

13. We are not fit to lead an army on the march unless we are familiar with the face of the country—its mountains and forests, its pitfalls and precipices, its marshes and swamps.

You must be sure that your team knows the lay of the land: what they should expect from an assigned judge on the case; the tendencies of an opposition expert who you have encountered before; statistical composition of the jury pool, etc. You don't want to micromanage or seem like you are, but you have to make sure your team is aware of relevant factors even if they are covered over lunch or an after-work beer, etc., to make it appear less overbearing.

14. We shall be unable to turn natural advantage to account unless we make use of local guides.

The flip side is that we have to realize that we don't know what we don't know. We need to not presume facts of the terrain and talk to other lawyers who may have seen and had prior dealings with an expert or judge. In Iowa there are ninety-nine counties, and it seems that each one has its own local rules. You need to ask your team, or other lawyers you are friendly with, if they have information on key terrain that we may not realize we don't know. Not only may local judges have proclivities that can seriously impact your case, but even the clerk or jury coordinator may have a special procedure that may affect how you present evidence, etc.

15. In war, practice dissimulation, and you will succeed.

In your efforts to explore the terrain and get information about what you feel you need to know, you must not tip off your opponent to what you are seeking out. You don't want to talk to a local lawyer about the local rules and then find out that lawyer is a cousin of your opponent or that they graduated in the same class at law school, as all of your enquiry information may be headed straight to your opponent.

16. Whether to concentrate or to divide your troops, must be decided by circumstances.

There will be times when you must know the strategic terrain but have to leave tactical terrain issues to your team. You can't know in war everything about a front line or battlefield. You certainly can know if a mass of rocks or wall will really offer cover or not. You can't know if an obstacle will cause an opponent to falter in an uphill charge. You will need to trust your team to make decisions about which part of a key location is the best spot to hold the point that you have deemed to be a can't-lose piece of terrain. Even with modern communication tools there will be times when you can't be in a position to view the terrain and will have to let your team member make a judgement call.

In World War II the allies looked at maps of northern France when preparing for the D- day invasion. The maps showed the terrain from above, and it was not widely known just how thick or tall the hedgerows where in certain areas which led to numerous issues for the soldiers on the ground looking at things from a ground level perspective. You can't know everything as a boss of a legal team, and even as a prosecutor of a basic DUI case you can't know everything the officer saw that night. You must rely on them to give you a better understanding of the case, so be sure to talk to them and ask for as much input as you can get. Don't presume when you don't have to.

17. Let your rapidity be that of the wind, your compactness that of the forest.

Moving fast *and* staying together are critical to the operation of any team. Take advantage of technology and make sure the team is not afraid of you as a leader to reach out to you when needed. If your staff is afraid to reach out to you about a concern or possible error, then the error will fester and can become a truly unsalvageable problem.

18. In raiding and plundering be like fire, in immovability like a mountain.

The best cross examinations are often short and sharp as knife point. So too, when holding a spot, a clever witness or lawyer can offer an un-rebuttable statement that shuts down the other side's attack. Even an expert witness countering with a confident and popular retort of "that is a common misconception," can really shut down a crossing lawyer.

19. Let your plans be dark and impenetrable as night, and when you move, fall like a thunderbolt.

This is an oft repeated line as it sounds good among other reasons, but it is also a special section as it certainly applies to the practice of law. The legal profession requires disclosure, yet a big part of the art of the profession is to deliver that material in such a way as to comply with the law, and let the opponent know the strength of your case to the point that they would be more likely to consider a plea offer. At the same time, you can't give away your best material. so that if push comes to shove and trial arrives, they don't know everything about how you will strike at them. In order for your plans of attack to have the most impact, surprise is often a cornerstone.

Cases vary but points of attack are often located at a tactical level. You may want to hold back on a point in depositions, so the opponent is not as prepared to face your approach. Without covering the matter first, however, you run the risk of not having a witness locked in ahead of time, and if they are capable, it will be harder to box them in, etc. Too many young lawyers and even jurors expect a Perry-Mason moment from you where you destroy a witness beyond repair in a single blow. In reality this is often unrealistic. The best you should hope for is to lock up a witness with several questions and answers at depositions that, when used together, allow you to box the witness in at trial without them seeing the ultimate tactic coming or at least not being able to wiggle free from it. It is also a great tactic to get a string of small pieces, often from different witnesses, and then stringing them together for the first time in closing arguments so that they come together into a devastating point or argument.

20. When you plunder a countryside, let the spoil be divided amongst your men; when you capture new territory, cut it up into allotments for the benefit of the soldiery.

The client/state will take their settlement, but it is important to properly reward your team with a fair cut of winnings or a bonus when a big criminal case is won. For the team to be properly motivated from top to bottom, you need them to feel that they will be and have been properly compensated for their contributions. Sometimes a big supreme-court win may motivate them with only a great or famous precedent as their reward, but most of the time they will want to feel that they have a dog in the fight for a case bonus or an end-of-year bonus, etc.

21. Ponder and deliberate before you make a move.

In the heat of trial, you may be called upon to make a decision without any time to ponder it or even briefly confer with your team. As in the heat of battle this must, at times, happen and the more you prepared and made yourself familiar with case material, the more your brain will be ready in that situation. In all other matters you should take time to ponder and think about issues in depth. You must spend time with hypothetical possibilities as responses to your moves and choices. You must think about what you would do and then what your opponent would do and then your best response to that, and so on. There is a danger of over-analyzing a situation, but critical decisions require careful decision making. Analyzing a situation and knowing the law and the facts of your case as well as the parties in play must all be taken together and processed so that with the help of your experience and wisdom the factors can be properly calculated.

22. He will conquer who has learnt the artifice of deviation. Such is the art of maneuvering.

In the end it is not truth that wins the day. Innocent people can be convicted, and guilty people can be acquitted. Justice must be fought for by proper analyzation of situations great and small. You must not only know what direction to head with a case but also when to take the first step; when to bring out a key point whether it is on direct or cross, with your witness or the opponent's, whether you wait to bring up an issue until a certain opponent witness has already testified, whether you wait during questioning with a witness that a key point is made or wait until closings to string together several relatively innocuous facts until they are an unbreakable chain and strike a mighty blow when first fused together late in the process. There will be tasks and aspects of the case you have left in control of others on your team. You must get them ready ahead of time to act and react, just like in war, without being able to completely communicate with you. How the case plays out may make you switch paths during the trial itself. You can be so rooted to your plan that you don't see an opportunity that requires you change part of your plans.

23. The Book of Army Management says: On the field of battle, the spoken word does not carry far enough: hence the institution of gongs and drums. Nor can ordinary objects be seen clearly enough: hence the institution of banners and flags.

Communication technology has grown in ways that Sun Tzu never dreamed of. Often lawyers would pass notes to each other and jotted down a few words on a legal pad that they passed down the table. Ineffective lawyers may frantically scribble something and then shove it in front of another lawyer at the table alerting the jury to the lawyer's concern, or worse, their fear that what is going on is hurting the case. A subtle lawyer would make such a note and quietly pass it to the fellow attorney, etc. Now, with most lawyers having a laptop at their table, they can send a message with lightning speed and with perfect typed clarity, plus handwriting won't get in the way. Such tools should be used and used to good effect without throwing off another lawyer who receives a note while they are active in the courtroom. You don't want to break their stride with constant bubbles of messages popping up on their laptop.

24. Gongs and drums, banners and flags, are means whereby the ears and eyes of the host may be focused on one particular point.

The ability to communicate during the heat of battle is a great asset. Notes should not be sent constantly during a trial but rather only when it is very important. Too many notes will throw the other team member off their rhythm and flow, or it might affect their confidence.

25. The host thus forming a single united body, is it impossible either for the brave to advance alone, or for the cowardly to retreat alone. This is the art of handling large masses of men.

The team must be literally on the same page when it comes to focus or to save a member from missing a key moment or point that will be needed to carry the day. Being able to send a note or even a copy of an exhibit or the precise deposition page for impeachment, via your screens, with a necessary part noted is something equivalent in technological advances like rifling in a gun or repeat-fire weapons. They are a huge leap forward, and if you don't take advantage of the technology then you do a disservice to your client and doubly so if your opponent does take advantage of technological advances. Fumbling though a 300-page deposition trying to find the part you highlighted or marked with a clip, etc. can break your flow and weaken the effectiveness of the strike. If you deliver the blow quickly, you can leave the moment emblazoned on the Jury's memory all the way through deliberations.

26. In night-fighting, then, make much use of signal-fires and drums, and in fighting by day, of flags and banners, as a means of influencing the ears and eyes of your army.

Communicating in different situations will, of course, necessitate different tactics. If your team member is at a lectern or if they have already approached a witness, they may not have a laptop with them. If in dire straits, old-school signs or signals may be needed or the classic asking for a moment to confer may be required to get the team member's attention back. Such extreme techniques must be used infrequently to make sure the jury does not come to think there is a problem or issue not going your way, keeping mind the jurors usually don't know exactly what you wanted to happen at any given moment. Your team should at least discuss ahead of time what subtle signs or signals you will use. Placing a pen cap at the end of your table with a small cough to call attention back to the table, for example, may be the code-red sign for the lawyer at a lectern to ask for a moment to confer, etc., without drawing too much attention to the issue before the jury.

27. A whole army may be robbed of its spirit; a commander-in-chief may be robbed of his presence of mind.

Without the ability to communicate, a team leader may get unnerved. You can overreact but communicating too much will affect the flow and affect the confidence of the team when they do key tasks later in the proceedings. Other team members may see you micromanage a fellow team member in action, and it may zap their confidence as well. The team members may lose confidence and not have the ability to swiftly counter things during their time in front of the jury or when they are to assist you at a key moment. A demoralized team will falter. An unsteady leader will make mistakes.

28. Now a soldier's spirit is keenest in the morning; by noonday it has begun to flag; and in the evening, his mind is bent only on returning to camp.

Trial is exhausting, especially one that has gone on for some time. Keeping your team in fighting form is key. It sounds simplistic but making sure people get sleep and are balancing the workload with exercise, a nightcap, or mediation, or whatever else may be needed to keep people ready for each day. Unless there has been a great surprise, you should not let your team members overdo it each night with work. Although you are right to feel that the more work you put in can make the difference, that thought must be balanced with avoiding losing sleep and rest. Pouring over notes for the hundredth time will not help. Your team has spent months on the case and may still have to be reminded that they are ready.

29. A clever general, therefore, avoids an army when its spirit is keen, but attacks it when it is sluggish and inclined to return. This is the art of studying moods.

The mood of the jury should also be considered. Although they are never likely to be happy until they leave the courthouse, it is wise to consider this when you speak to them for opening or closing. Most people are more sluggish right after lunch or at the end of the day when they have one eye on the clock as they count down the last minutes of the day, for example. The longer the trial goes on, and often during the afternoon sessions, you can lose a juror's attention easily and you must remember to use a bit of thunder to let them know a key point is on the table.

30. Disciplined and calm, to await the appearance of disorder and hubbub amongst the enemy:—this is the art of retaining self-possession.

Although your team may run like a well-oiled machine, if you notice the opposition is disorganized, it certainly can help to make things worse for them with a well-timed objection or other tactic.

31. To be near the goal while the enemy is still far from it, to wait at ease while the enemy is toiling and struggling, to be well-fed while the enemy is famished:–this is the art of husbanding one's strength.

Having your team be confident and paced while they watch an opponent scramble or rush can be a huge morale boost for your people. They will feel ready and confident about your team's chances and more certain of the value of preparing.

32. To refrain from intercepting an enemy whose banners are in perfect order, to refrain from attacking an army drawn up in calm and confident array:–this is the art of studying circumstances.

Take advantage of disorder, and if you see order then you may want to wait to strike in a certain way until later when things are more in your favor. If you see that they are in poor form, you may want to change up the order of your witnesses to take advantage. You can bring in a weaker witness who may do better at that time or a stronger witness who will keep them faltering.

33. It is a military axiom not to advance uphill against the enemy, nor to oppose him when he comes downhill.

If you can avoid hitting them when they have momentum and are on a roll, then do so. You may want to attack to keep their streak of forward positive movement from growing in momentum. You want to stop them if they have great flow and are scoring points, but you have to be careful to not offer more fuel for their fire of success. A great aspect of the case that is key to your success may be dulled at certain points and enhanced at others. You don't want to let the opponent run rampant without being checked at all, but you must choose the impact on your goals and the timing of opportunities. If you can just toss out a few objections and break flow, then great. If you have to raise a key point that you want the jury to remember, it may not be worth using that if it may get buried by the other side's momentum.

34. Do not pursue an enemy who simulates flight; do not attack soldiers whose temper is keen.

Don't get baited into a trap. This is not a revolutionary idea, but it must be noted. There are many ways an opponent or an opponent witness can try to bait you into a mistake. Be careful and stay on your targets. Don't let a witness bait you with an answer such as "well that depends," or "I can't answer that truthfully with a just a yes or no." If you choose to explore the reason for their answer, it can lead to a great moment for their witness. Be prepared how to deal with every expert's favorite tool of "well that is a common misconception," etc.

35. Do not swallow bait offered by the enemy. Do not interfere with an army that is returning home.

You shouldn't miss out on an impromptu chance to score an unplanned point, but all is fair in love, war, and trial, so be mindful of the ground you are on. If an opponent is retreating on a point and then you overreach to stop them, or rub it in, so to speak, you can end up overextending yourself and giving them a way back in. If you are certain you got what you wanted from the opponent's expert, then move on.

36. When you surround an army, leave an outlet free. Do not press a desperate foe too hard.

Most would say, crush the opponent. In war there are resources that may be important to keep, but in trial, especially for the client, it is all about the now and winning as much as possible. That being said, it can seem harsh to some jurors to see you crush a witness. In their novice eyes you can quickly go from a great lawyer who advances a lot of with what you say to just an asshole who can't be trusted after harsh treatment of a witness. You are going to want them to still 'like you' and trust you when you are making your 'ask' in closings.

37. Such is the art of warfare.

It is the art. Every case or battlefield is very different, so we can't predict how to handle things in general, as variables will affect each case differently. Only through studying the art can you better develop your ability to see it with clarity in the moment of truth.

VIII. Variation in Tactics

1. Sun Tzu said: In war, the general receives his commands from the sovereign, collects his army and concentrates his forces.

You will have your goal from the client that they will set as a 'win'. Then you will put your team together; lawyers, staff and your own expert witnesses, etc. You will decide the key points that must be presented or held on to at all costs, to get the jury to believe your explanation of the case and why they should rule in your favor. It can be said that everything you do over years of litigating one case will have happened so that you can literally say a handful of key words in closing.

2. When in difficult country, do not encamp. In country where high roads intersect, join hands with your allies. Do not linger in dangerously isolated positions. In hemmed-in situations, you must resort to stratagem. In desperate position, you must fight.

Don't encamp to low ground if you are dealing with an area that must be addressed with a witness; if it is a strong point for the opponent, then do so and get out of it as fast as possible. Don't dwell on their strengths. Get what you need or at least what you can, and get out of that area and redirect the jury back to a strength of yours as soon as you can.

In communicating ground, unite with allies. In cases where you have co-defendants, you should do what you can to coordinate your efforts if you feel you can trust them. You have to decide if you can trust the lawyer for a co-defendant or if they may seem trustworthy, but under orders from their client they might change directions and turn on you.

Don't linger in wide open isolated ground. As with low disadvantageous ground, don't dwell too long on your weaker topics in closing. You have either crushed their point or weakened it. If you have only done some damage, then it may still be worth talking about but if you still feel it is a strong point for your opponent, then deal with it as best you can and move on. Often you leave such material for the middle of your closing and not the start or end, as those resonate with the jury and stay longer in their minds, especially in complex cases.

When hemmed-in, strategy must be employed to save yourself. When the lay of the land offers natural obstructions or limitations for your positions, then you must employ strategic decisions to maximize your results and minimize your exposure. A proficient opponent expert witness or police officer won't likely just roll over and give you what you want, so you will need to plan ahead with impeachment options that they can't wiggle out of or a long string of innocuous questions that you string together to make a valid point before they see where you are going. You can't always pick the battlefield in war, and similarly you can't pick who the opponent uses for experts or other non lay witnesses. If you're defending a client in a criminal case, you may have drawn a good officer who was called to the scene or handled the investigation. The lab tech, coroner, or other expert that the state chooses may be one of the better ones they have in their employ. You must deal with that terrain as it presents itself and adjust accordingly. Of course, your chances to weaken your opponent will be in large part based on knowing about them up front, so you know how to best prepare at trial. You are not ready to face them until you have done your research, not just on the subject area but on your opponent as well.

When cornered on desperate ground, you have no choice but to fight. Sometimes, of course, the terrain or situation or witness will simply be strong and without relative weakness, yet you must not let what they have to offer to the jury go unchecked. In this desperate state you will have to rely on your ability to strike at the witness and weaken their position. If you can leave the jury with some doubt of their otherwise valid contributions, that may be the best you can hope for. Only your individual skill and talent will enable you to get something out of a desperate situation where you must attack out of necessity, without an easy or natural opening. Here scoring points will attest to your abilities. The state/client will only care about the overall win or loss, but when you accomplish something in these difficult circumstances, it can still help greatly. Dunking a basketball over a second-grader is no test of skill for an adult. To be able to score against an NBA player at a local pickup game is likely worth mentioning for the average adult.

3. There are roads which must not be followed, armies which must be not attacked, towns which must be besieged, positions which must not be contested, commands of the sovereign which must not be obeyed.

There is a difference between a desperate ground and an insurmountable approach that should not be taken, regardless of how much skill you have. A great enemy of a general or lawyer is their ego. Don't get so full of yourself that you fail to see a point that can't be won, or worse, that your attack will just draw more attention to the opponent's strength in front of the jury. The last thing you want is to attack a point and have a witness hold up well and come away seeming even more credible to the jury on an issue, as that may carry over to every point they have to offer.

4. The general who thoroughly understands the advantages that accompany variation of tactics knows how to handle his troops.

You need to know when and if to push a point, and if the fight is to be gruesome should *you* do it or another member of your team. Some lawyers employ a team member to deal with impossible positions, not because they may pull it off, but rather so that a weaker member of your team draws the ire of the jury, and hopefully the taint or stain of that loss will not stick to the primary lawyers, especially the ones that will make the closing arguments.

5. The general who does not understand these, may be well acquainted with the configuration of the country, yet he will not be able to turn his knowledge to practical account.

Wins in court come from success on all fronts, or as many as possible, to carry the day. It is not enough to know how to offer great closings and openings. It is not enough to be better than the other side at objections and pre-trial-motion practice. It is not enough to have personality, likeability, and charisma that plays well with a jury. It is not enough to know the case facts backwards and forwards in great detail. You must be able to have as many of these as possible, if not all, to achieve victory. Victory is all the state/client knows at the end as to what you did for them, lest they should think you failed them.

6. So, the student of war who is unversed in the art of war of varying his plans, even though he be acquainted with the Five Advantages, will fail to make the best use of his men.

You must continuously work to be adept at all aspects of what is needed from a trial lawyer or at least have a team that incorporates all these required areas.

7. Hence in the wise leader's plans, considerations of advantage and of disadvantage will be blended together.

Although one juror may say after a trial that 'X' was critical to them, another juror who joined in the verdict may attribute the win to a completely different reason. The win may come from your efforts to weaken an opponent's expert witness, or it may come from the strength of your evidence and argument, etc. You must not only study the case and be ready on all aspects, you must also tie it all together so that twelve different individuals with different perspectives and backgrounds come together and rule in your favor. There will not likely be one key point or fact that carries the day for all twelve, so you must push forward numerous points per case. All aspects of the case will come together at the end so that the trial is won. What will carry the day is knowing what to push and what to target.

8. If our expectation of advantage be tempered in this way, we may succeed in accomplishing the essential part of our schemes.

Advantages are things that stick with the jury toward your favor. You must look at what you have and will be able to show to these twelve strangers. You need to know what they care about. Knowing the proclivities of jurors and how their backgrounds may skew them toward one direction or thought and another will be key material you will acquire during jury section. Years of work may need to be altered at the last minute based on the makeup of the jury. The study of trial law is therefore also the study of the terrain of the jurors. There is a reason, of course, why whole books and treatises focus on jury selection and jury 'understanding'. Human nature and the background of the jurors as individuals will determine what is weak and strong in your case. Jurors will act based on their experience as well as current trends in the news, such as political developments or the world of entertainment. Their upbringing as well as current events will be great predictors on what they will think.

9. If, on the other hand, in the midst of difficulties we are always ready to seize an advantage, we may extricate ourselves from misfortune.

The winner of a case is not always the 'right' side. Many prosecutors have joked that convicting a guilty person is easy but convicting an innocent person is so much harder. A defendant can be convicted when they are innocent. A guilty person, who committed a crime may, escape with reasonable doubt fairly being seen by a jury. Comparative fault's impact on a jury award may be skewed by factors that should not have stuck with the jury. They are people and often are far less intelligent than you may want. You also have to see the world as they do, i.e. as people who only have a cursory knowledge of the law and certainly have not immersed themselves in the particulars of our complex laws for decades as lawyers have. A lawyer may pull off a win against the current of law because the current of the human animal enabled them to employ a strategy that wins, when maybe it should not have.

10. Reduce the hostile chiefs by inflicting damage on them; and make trouble for them and keep them constantly engaged; hold out specious allurements and make them rush to any given point.

Our system is adversarial. To offer the opponent a red herring or other false enticement is by most accounts within the bounds of the system. Tactics such as discovery dumps that seem to make it harder to find a key document for the opponent or letting it be known to a clerk that you fear a certain witness is weak when they are strong, in the hopes it gets back to the opponent, are known to have met with success. Talking about concerns of a certain potential juror at you team's table loudly enough for the other side to hear, or even something as juvenile as talking about the judge liking a certain sports team when they do not, in the hopes that the other side will try to engage in small talk with the judge favorable

to that team. Such things cost you nothing but can create disorder
or discomfort in your opponent.

11. The art of war teaches us to rely not on the likelihood of
the enemy's not coming, but on our own readiness to receive
him; not on the chance of his not attacking, but rather on the
fact that we have made our position unassailable.

The best way to protect yourself from effective opponent
strategies or dirty tricks is to make sure that what you have to
offer to the jury through exhibits, witnesses, and argument is as
solid as can be. There is no absolute position or argument that
can't be undone. Jurors can often latch on to illogical positions
that fly in the face of hundreds of other jurors' positions. I recall
a DUI trial when I was still a prosecutor where, although neither
side ever argued it, a seventy five year old juror arrived at the
conclusion of the defendant's intoxication based almost solely on
the presence of an open can of Red Bull, as she thought it was
alcoholic. It is the nature of our profession that it is not an exact
science but all that can be done is to bolster positions as much
as we are able to. It is our zealous duty to do so to minimize the
chances of such anomalies.

12. There are five dangerous faults which may affect a general:
(1) Recklessness, which leads to destruction; (2) cowardice,
which leads to capture; (3) a hasty temper, which can be
provoked by insults; (4) a delicacy of honor which is sensitive
to shame; (5) over-solicitude for his men, which exposes him
to worry and trouble.

1.   Recklessness is a great danger for a general or lawyer. Being
overconfident to the point of feeling that you don't need to give
everything you have, has brought down many great generals and
lawyers in situations when they should have prevailed. Proceeding
on a path that arises out of a surprise at trial when you are not ready
and have not planned for the sudden change is reckless. Asking

questions that you don't know the answer to, and can't impeach the witness to correct, is reckless. You must prepare for likely, and not likely, variables if you are to be ready to deal with any situation that may arise.

2.   Cowardice can be the opposite of recklessness. If you don't ask a question that could help, as you feel that your impeachment won't be strong enough, etc., is cowardice detrimental to the case. Being afraid to slightly deviate or alter your plans in trial when faced with an obvious change that you can deal with, is cowardice. It may feel alarming to change from a course that you have spent months or years preparing for. There is no shame in being surprised by something you couldn't have truly seen coming, but you must deal with surprises and not ignore the impact they have on your existing plans.

3.   In the wonderful translation of the *Art of War* by Samuel Griffith,[3] the author points out the great example of Tsang Chih and his use of temper to gain a strategic advantage. In summary, the wise general was defending a city to a far superior force that was arriving. A portion of his opponent's army had reached the city gates and it was accepted norm of the day for the generals to exchange gifts and pleasantries. Tsang Chih broke with the tradition and sent over a bottle that seemed to hold an expensive wine when in reality it contained his own urine. This enraged the attacking general so much that, instead of managing his army and waiting for all of his force to arrive, he began to attack with what he had at the moment. This was not near enough to attack a walled city. As his troops slowly arrived at to the front, they were sent in to attack by the enraged attacker, piece meal. And they were subsequently annihilated by the defenders. So much so that it was said that then the last waive of attackers

---

³ Samuel B. Griffith, *Sun Tzu the Art of War* (Oxford University Press, Oxford: 1963)

sought to climb the walls, they did not need ladders as they could just climb up the corpses of the attackers that had come before them. This one act and use of anger lead to the attackers losing an easy fight and altered the course of a war and of a nation for years to come.

4. Your future reputation matters not at all to the state/client. They will never understand that you may not want to look one way or another in front of your colleagues. They may not even care about your ethical obligations and what will happen to your ability to practice law in the future, based on an action you can take on their behalf now. Of course, the risk of losing your license, and following the state bar's rules, must guide you. Saving face with a judge you will likely see again or an opposition lawyer who perhaps you went to law school with, etc. is not to be a factor that should affect your representation of this client in this matter.

5. Excessive worrying about the mental and physical wellbeing of your troops will hurt you. There must be some sacrifice on behalf of the state. That is, theoretically, what the money is for, your time and exertions. Robert E. Lee is purported to have said "To be a good soldier, you must love the army. To be a good commander, you must be willing to order the death of the thing you love."[4] A trial can be the cumulation of months or years of your work. You can't worry about one of your team members having their feelings hurt, if at the last minute you feel a need to pull them off of a witness that they had been set to handle, etc. Again, the client will not care about your team camaraderie after the case is over. You have to do what is needed to get the job done even if you offend some of your team. They should understand that it is not personal and that you must do what you think is best

---

[4] Michael Shaara, *The Killer Angels: The Classic Novel of the Civil War* (Ballantine Books, New York: 1996)

to win the case for the client. Law is a profession that calls for us to be professional at all times.

13. These are the five besetting sins of a general, ruinous to the conduct of war.

It is our nature to let our past success go to our head and to be proud of our past accomplishments. While you may have a proper right to be proud, you can't let pride or your temper or bad blood with an opponent from a past case affect your judgment and decision in this case. You will do all you can to try to make sure you win your case, but you have to also make sure that it is not your flaws that cause a defeat.

14. When an army is overthrown and its leader slain, the cause will surely be found among these five dangerous faults. Let them be a subject of meditation.

If you truly and honestly analyze your past defeats, you will see many if not all these factors present.

IX. The Army on the March

1. Sun Tzu said: We come now to the question of encamping the army, and observing signs of the enemy. Pass quickly over mountains, and keep in the neighborhood of valleys.

As the case moves along place yourself in positions that enable you to defend yourself and to attack if you see an advantage. Things can happen quickly, so make sure to exploit advantages as they appear.

2. Camp in high places, facing the sun. Do not climb heights in order to fight. So much for mountain warfare.

There are positions that can, by their nature, give you advantages, the 'high ground', as it were. In law you have to be mindful of motion deadlines and other restrictions that, if not addressed, will cause you unnecessary harm. You should also hold the opponent to task on such things, as any such advantages culled from their flaws should be taken. Whenever possible, fight for an advantageous venue. Don't underestimate the difficulty of working out of a hotel against your opponent at depositions and trial, etc.

3. After crossing a river, you should get far away from it.

Once you have overcome obstacles that can endanger you, then you should expeditiously move away from them so as not to fall back into a susceptible position where your choices are limited.

4. When an invading force crosses a river in its onward march, do not advance to meet it in mid-stream. It will be best to let half the army get across, and then deliver your attack.

In the alternative, observe your opponent's movements and note when you have a great time to advance on them. Pick good times to strike when they are disorganized and divided in their focus. When there is an obstacle that slows them down, you can strike when they can't bring all of their force to bare. If the opponent law firm is engaged in a large suit or trial with another party, find out when that matter is heating up, and choose that time to file motions in your case with them.

5. If you are anxious to fight, you should not go to meet the invader near a river which he has to cross.

You must not only watch their positions but where they will soon be or must go, to anticipate when a good time to strike will be in the future. It pays to be friends with the scheduling clerk so that you can learn when an opponent is going to trial on another matter or has an appeal deadline due soon, as you know then that they will be busy on other matters.

6. Moor your craft higher up than the enemy, and facing the sun. Do not move up-stream to meet the enemy. So much for river warfare.

Be sure that you don't have to swim upstream to get where you need to be. Be mindful of your team's own obligations and avoid your team getting overwhelmed with obligations on various fronts.

7. In crossing saltmarshes, your sole concern should be to get over them quickly, without any delay.

You have to avoid getting bogged down in one case that allows you to not give proper attention to others. You also must be sure not to get stuck obsessing over one area of your case and not give attention to other areas that need attention.

8. If forced to fight in a saltmarsh, you should have water and grass near you, and get your back to a clump of trees. So much for operations in salt-marches.

Even in disadvantageous positions there can be least bad places to fight. When dealing with a dangerous topic that can't be ignored, you may have an uphill battle, so to speak, but you can choose from which angle you go up the hill to challenge the opponent's strength. When crossing the opponent expert, for example, you get to choose how you approach them and how you will defend your side's argument from an opponent's position. Pick your angle or approach and keep the witness dealing with you on the point of the ground that you choose.

9. In dry, level country, take up an easily accessible position with rising ground to your right and on your rear, so that the danger may be in front, and safety lie behind. So much for campaigning in flat country.

When you choose to attack, you must be sure you are truly on solid ground and not exposed in some way to an easy counter. This is a good time to consider not asking the dreaded 'one-too-many' questions or ignoring a point that lets the opponent get a strong and concise re-direct in the jury's mind, or a recross that takes the sting out of your strike.

10. These are the four useful branches of military knowledge which enabled the Yellow Emperor to vanquish four several sovereigns.
Only by embracing these variables and reviewing them in every case will you get to the point when you can effortlessly but continuously consider them as the case progresses.

11. All armies prefer high ground to low and sunny places to dark.

Your team will have places and points they see as strong. If you don't focus on them or deal with them enough, your team will be nervous and lose confidence. Although you pick the path forward, if you don't address what they think as key flaws and drive home the team's preferred strong points, they will be nervous.

12. If you are careful of your men, and camp on hard ground, the army will be free from disease of every kind, and this will spell victory.

Just as you may hope for your opponent's team members to be stretched too far to be at their best, you must do what you can, and take care of your people to make sure their mental and physical health is maintained, so they can be at their best for the critical moments of your cases. Don't underestimate how a long trial can weaken your team and the client's health both mentally and physically.

13. When you come to a hill or a bank, occupy the sunny side, with the slope on your right rear. Thus, you will at once act for the benefit of your soldiers and utilize the natural advantages of the ground.

The team will be alarmed if you don't take advantage of what seems to be naturally in your favor. Again, communication in your team as to what is the overall plan is important. They may be loyal and have worked with you for a long time, but if they don't see where you are going and why, they may get restless.

14. When, in consequence of heavy rains up-country, a river which you wish to ford is swollen and flecked with foam, you must wait until it subsides.

Situations change. Things that you may be able to do on one occasion you may not be able to do at other times. You can't overextend or try to do what you normally do if you have too many cases going on at once, or if you are down staff due to illness or turnover. Just because you were able to tackle a similar project in the past, does not mean that this time it will work out the same favorable way using the same efforts. Know your realistic limits and don't overextend. You can't risk one client's case by taking on too many other cases that reduce your ability to meet the needs of your existing clients.

15. Country in which there are precipitous cliffs with torrents running between, deep natural hollows, confined places, tangled thickets, quagmires and crevasses, should be left with all possible speed and not approached.

There are certain types of case that come with certain difficulties. For example, a defense attorney in a domestic assault case will likely have to cross exam a sympathetic victim. There is no way to avoid some types of difficulties in certain cases. Sometimes you can't avoid a terrain that can be treacherous for the best of advocates. That being said, you should pick members of your team accordingly. A female lawyer will seem less evil cross examining a female victim, etc. Such harsh realities can't and shouldn't be ignored.

16. While we keep away from such places, we should get the enemy to approach them; while we face them, we should let the enemy have them on his rear.

If you have a sympathetic victim or other naturally favorable witness or evidence, you should play it up as much as possible. To do right by your client, you must push whatever advantage you are given by the natural terrain or from any other source. Current trends in employee relations should not have total control of your choices, and the team should understand that you are doing what is best for the case and the client when you make certain tactical decisions about your team.

17. If in the neighborhood of your camp there should be any hilly country, ponds surrounded by aquatic grass, hollow basins filled with reeds, or woods with thick undergrowth, they must be carefully routed out and searched; for these are places where men in ambush or insidious spies are likely to be lurking.

Traps are a fact of litigation, whether they are set by a clever opponent witness during cross or a deposition, or an unnoticed foundational issue with a key piece of evidence. There is a reason why such things are called surprises. You have to look for them in all the proverbial usual places where such things may be hidden. Knowing where to look and try to catch these possible ambushes is part of the art of practicing law. Being aware and in the moment as well as being prepared and well versed with the facts of the case are your best tools to be ready to deal with a possible ambush.

18. When the enemy is close at hand and remains quiet, he is relying on the natural strength of his position.

In all kinds of contexts such as negotiations, it is often said to be prudent to let the other side make the first offer. The theory is that if they ask for too much you reject it and if they offer a better deal then you thought they would, it can be an indicator of how they feel about their chances, etc. If they are holding and waiting for you to come to them, then they may feel that you will offer favorable terms. If they are holding and not moving at all, then it is always for a reason; perhaps they can't find a great angle of attack or they feel their best choice is to wait and use what they have. In war the number of resources to launch an attack exceeds what is needed to defend. The same is true in litigation.

19. When he keeps aloof and tries to provoke a battle, he is anxious for the other side to advance.

An opponent may try to draw you out when they can't determine your strategy or strongest points. At other times they may seek to use depositions to try to figure out what your long game is. As has been already covered here, you must find the right delicate balance between showing your strength to merit a good offer while not disclosing your best attacks to your opponent who would then have all the time they would want, and need, to spend on countering.

20. If his place of encampment is easy of access, he is tendering a bait.

If you see an obvious target that your opponents are not protecting, it may be that the target has a natural protection you can't see, such as an unusually strong victim, for example, who will testify well and hold up well.

21. Movement amongst the trees of a forest shows that the enemy is advancing. The appearance of a number of screens in the midst of thick grass means that the enemy wants to make us suspicious.

Even if you do not wish to employ deception, you still have to be able to see it coming at you. There are certain things that you must be aware of to anticipate an attack. You have to look for tells from witnesses and lawyers that you notice in repeated cases and act on them. Even as small a sign of a lawyer picking up their binder or unlatching it to retrieve a document could be a tip that they feel they are about to be able to impeach.

22. The rising of birds in their flight is the sign of an ambuscade. Startled beasts indicate that a sudden attack is coming.

You must look for signs and indicators from your opponent that let you know a moment of consequence is coming. It may be a great time to object which may throw them off in a moment when they should be flowing smoothly toward a critical strike.

23. When there is dust rising in a high column, it is the sign of chariots advancing; when the dust is low, but spread over a wide area, it betokens the approach of infantry. When it branches out in different directions, it shows that parties have been sent to collect firewood. A few clouds of dust moving to and fro signify that the army is encamping.

Trials are often pushed back numerous times during the litigation process on a case. You need to look for signs that the opponent is finally ready, and make sure you are, too. For example, learning from the clerk that your opponent has other matters that have been moved in connection to your ongoing case is a good sign.

24. Humble words and increased preparations are signs that the enemy is about to advance. Violent language and driving forward as if to the attack are signs that he will retreat.

An opponent who is confident in an attack, rarely feels a need to boast about it. If they are confident, they will often remain quiet in the knowledge their plans are superior. If they have doubts, then they may bluster in the hopes it makes you back down and they don't need to attack that point. This is an important instance of knowing your opponent's personality.

25. When the light chariots come out first and take up a position on the wings, it is a sign that the enemy is forming for battle.

No question presented to your witness or theirs should be without purpose. You have to pay attention to the questions and answers *and* what they purport. Where is that lawyer going with a given line of questioning? If you know where it is going, and it will hurt you, then object or try to alter the course when you can. You should also be prepared to deal with the damaging material on cross. The plan is that you will already know what they have to offer and how you will attack it, but don't discount new ways as you go. You may see a quip or turn of phrase that you can throw back at the witness in your cross that was not part of your original plans.

26. Peace proposals unaccompanied by a sworn covenant indicate a plot.

Late plea offers may simply be a tactic to get you to waste time while the enemy knows that they are committed to fight to the end.

27. When there is much running about and the soldiers fall into rank, it means that the critical moment has come.

If at this time your preparations are not in place, then it may be too late. It is always better to be ready for trial only for it to be moved than to not be ready when trial begins. Yes, this will mean extra time for you to prepare for each possible trial date but that is part of your duty to your client.

28. When some are seen advancing and some retreating, it is a lure.

Be mindful of the opponent who feigns disorder but truly has their people ready. For example, in jurisdictions the have electronic filing systems you should check to see if the returns of subpoenas are on file.

29. When the soldiers stand leaning on their spears, they are faint from want of food.

If you have a pretrial meeting shortly before a trial date, it is wise to observe your opponents. Do they seem organized and ready or are they struggling and looking for documents that should be at the ready? Do they seem disheveled and tired? This may show they have been doing recent or not enough prep work.

30. If those who are sent to draw water begin by drinking themselves, the army is suffering from thirst.

Look for clues that their team or their client are tiring of the conflict, as it may be a good time to reach a worthwhile deal before the fight proceeds.

31. If the enemy sees an advantage to be gained and makes no effort to secure it, the soldiers are exhausted.

If your opponent misses an opportunity that you thought they would take, it can be a sign that they are either not as proficient as they should be, that they are exhausted or overwhelmed by the weight of the matter and are not paying attention to details.

32. If birds gather on any spot, it is unoccupied. Clamor by night betokens nervousness.

After a year or longer litigation, should you or the opponent still need to work late into the night on the last night before trial to finish your preparation? I would say 'no' if you have used your time wisely, but it is hard thing to not do. There are always little tweaks or some last-minute double checks that your nerves may want you to look at, just in case. However, often a mistake or error found late during a trial may be something for which there is no time to fix it due to disclosure rules or travel logistics, etc. The odds that you catch a major error the night before trial are slim to none and a good night's rest is also very valuable.

33. If there is disturbance in the camp, the general's authority is weak. If the banners and flags are shifted about, sedition is afoot. If the officers are angry, it means that the men are weary.

Anytime you see disorder in your opponent's team, it is a good sign that they are not on the same page or that they are not in agreement with how to proceed and are at best doing so begrudgingly. This of course can be a great time to attack if you are able to.

34. When an army feeds its horses with grain and kills its cattle for food, and when the men do not hang their cooking-pots over the campfires, showing that they will not return to their tents, you may know that they are determined to fight to the death.

People always talk. The legal community is small, even in larger cities. If you keep your network of contacts going, it is not hard to learn about the morale of an opponent or to see how they are making out with the firm's expenses when they have a lot invested in a given case. Many firms will take out loans to fund large cases and the fear of not being able to pay those off, if they lose, can be a big incentive for a lawyer to want their client to take a deal.

When on the hunt for information, you should not discount the return value that you can get by simply bringing donuts to the scheduling clerks.

35. The sight of men whispering together in small knots or speaking in subdued tones points to disaffection amongst the rank and file.

During the litigation or even the trial itself, you can notice and detect animosity within the opponent's legal team. A key team member may choose to move on to a new firm or other direction that can weaken your opponent. During trial, if their animosity boils over, it is not uncommon for lawyers to show their internal discord during hearings outside the presence of the jury or even in front of the jury. If even the legal team is not sure of the case, why should the jury believe what they have to say?

36. Too frequent rewards signify that the enemy is at the end of his resources; too many punishments betray a condition of dire distress.

In war a soldier that abandons their post can be court-marshaled and face death. Unfortunately, there are no such penalties in law. If a junior team member leaves a firm at any time, then there is not much recourse to be had. The ethics and conflict rules will prevent them from relating information to the other side. If a lawyer tries to abandon their client, especially close to trial, then that lawyer could face sanction from the Bar, but other than that a lawyer can generally leave whenever they want to. If you are too hard on your team, you may lose a member at an inopportune time. Most rewards are contingent upon staying until after the big win, but a firm at the end of their credit with pending litigation can show numerous signs of faltering that are a big tip that a settlement your opponent had previously not entertained would now be available.

37. To begin by bluster, but afterwards to take fright at the enemy's numbers, shows a supreme lack of intelligence.

You want to show the strength of your case when trying to convince the other side to offer you a deal, but you don't want to seem desperate or claim an unrealistic picture of strength that the other side can see is false. To do that will show that you are desperate to settle due to weakness, known or unknown, to the opponent. In trial, don't brag or make a big production of telling the jury you will have a big point or show a key weakness in the opponent's case and then you don't or just bring them something not nearly as remarkable. This will destroy your credibility with the jury.

38. When envoys are sent with compliments in their mouths, it is a sign that the enemy wishes for a truce.

When going to the other side with a plea offer, especially after a long and protracted litigation, you need to choose your words carefully. If you are too brash or point to unrealistic estimates of your strengths, then your opponent will presume you to be weak. If you are too conciliatory, then you also will appear to be in position of insufficient strength. It is far better to offer a clear and realistic picture of your strengths and your opponent's weaknesses. If you tell them things that they can see are false, then they were not really strengths or weaknesses to begin with.

39. If the enemy's troops march up angrily and remain facing ours for a long time without either joining battle or taking themselves off again, the situation is one that demands great vigilance and circumspection.

If the enemy is drawn up for an attack but does not follow through, it can be a sign of many things. They may have concern about their plans. They may feel their strong position will force you to withdraw even before the attack without risk of actual battle. If they are ready for the fight but pause, it may be that the opponent is bringing another force to bear to add to their odds, and caution should be employed. You have seen all you can gather about your case, so you must do your best to look at the individual situation and make your estimates as best you can, so you can make the best-informed decision you can.

40. If our troops are no more in number than the enemy, that is amply sufficient; it only means that no direct attack can be made. What we can do is simply to concentrate all our available strength, keep a close watch on the enemy, and obtain reinforcements.

Numbers in war do not guarantee a win. In law you may have a stronger case, but the variables can still shift the outcome. Be it an odd holdout juror or a witness who uncharacteristically does not have their 'A' game, or nightmare of all nightmares, an opponent strategy that you did not adequately prepare for; things can always happen to alter the outcome of an unwinnable case. You have to keep in mind that the original Twinkie defense persuaded a jury! In 1979, a former elected official argued to a jury at trial that when he came into the San Francisco city hall and killed the mayor and a fellow elected official named Harvey Milk, he did so under the influence of bad food. He claimed that he had been a very healthy eater all his life but due to financial problems he started eating large quantities of junk food and that made him not think clearly when he shot two people. Although not specifically argued as a defense term, the defense did note diminished capacity could be noticed by his changes in habits like eating junk food after years of very healthy eating and that he was on a sugar rush at the time of the murder.[5]

41. He who exercises no forethought but makes light of his opponents is sure to be captured by them.

It is not enough to make plans. You must put yourself in your opponent's shoes and anticipate what they will do to counter your attacks and to strike back. You must see your weak points, as they will be seen by the opponent and the jury, and prepare for the counter moves. You must also make your plans with what you anticipate your opponent's plans to be. Your plans will not be executed in a vacuum but rather they will be tested with variables of jurors and judges assigned to the case and, of course, with a team of lawyers on the other side doing everything they can to stop you. You must be ever mindful that you have an educated and experienced opponent who is trying to stop you and who may very well be operating with the theory that their team won't eat or be able to feed their family, so to speak, unless they beat you. Prison or millions of dollars are on the line; there is much to fight for, and the stakes can be very high for the clients and lawyers.

42. If soldiers are punished before they have grown attached to you, they will not prove submissive; and, unless submissive, then will be practically useless. If, when the soldiers have become attached to you, punishments are not enforced, they will still be unless.

Just as the morale of your enemy will tell you when to offer a good settlement, you must also keep your team well motivated

---

[5] See https://www.oxfordreference.com/display/10.1093/oi/
authority.20110803110351486

and working diligently. When a soldier takes action in war, they may do so as they want to stay alive. When your staff works, they want to be compensated. The notion of justice will only motivate a lawyer to burn the midnight oil so much. There must be something in for them such as a bonus or partnership track, etc. Keep the motivations clear and don't welch on any promised rewards.

43. Therefore, soldiers must be treated in the first instance with humanity but kept under control by means of iron discipline. This is a certain road to victory.

Your team must truly earn what they are promised. If they are handling their assignments regarding the case in a half-assed fashion, then get rid of them. You can attract better lawyers for your firm if you are worthy. If you have rewarded your team too much or too soon, they may take their foot off the gas. Last year's associate who is now a junior partner may not be willing to do as much as they did before. In big cases you can't do it all yourself, as much as you may want to. If you are doing too much, then that can lead to the quality of your work being compromised.

44. If in training soldiers commands are habitually enforced, the army will be well-disciplined; if not, its discipline will be bad.

If one member of your team feels that they are asked to do more work than others without more compensation, that will kill morale. If they see that you have a favorite who is treated better than others, that will be remembered by members in the team longer than any kindness you may have done for them. You must treat each team member consistently based on what you have done for them in the past, and you can't be kinder or gentler to one member and not others.

45. If a general shows confidence in his men but always insists on his orders being obeyed, the gain will be mutual.

You may like your team; you may even feel like a parent or mentor or protegee towards them, but you have to do what must be done for the war, not because you do or don't like some team members on your staff. You may want to give a big break to one of your team that has earned it, but you can't take a chance on them hitting a goal at the risk of the client's case. The client will not care about how your team gets along after the case is over if a team member was trying their best when they made a critical error. They want to win and want you to do whatever gives them the best chance of getting a win, period.

X. Terrain

1. Sun Tzu said: We may distinguish six kinds of terrain, to wit: (1) Accessible ground; (2) entangling ground; (3) temporizing ground; (4) narrow passes; (5) precipitous heights; (6) positions at a great distance from the enemy.

2. Ground which can be freely traversed by both sides is called accessible.

There are topics that will offer pros and cons for both sides. In a conflict there will be ground that is not particularly disadvantageous or advantageous for either side but may yet encourage both sides to fight on. Most cases that go to trial are close to begin with. Victory may be achieved by simply how well you argue a point or aspect of the case that could have been used by either side.

3. With regard to ground of this nature, be before the enemy in occupying the raised and sunny spots, and carefully guard your line of supplies. Then you will be able to fight with advantage.

There are types of areas that you will both want to reach. For example, in front of a jury you know that, in a DUI case, a defendant's alleged refusal to take a breath test will be mentioned.

You know that the state prosecutor will want to address it and argue why would a person who knows they are sober not take the test? If you are the defense lawyer, then you should not let that thought linger very long. You can talk about it in your opening and make sure that the jury has heard examples of why a person may refuse, such as issues with the device or poor explanation of the process by the officer, etc. You should not leave such a topic unaddressed.

4. Ground which can be abandoned but is hard to re-occupy is called entangling.

There are tactical and strategic advantages that you may want to choose to back away from or ignore for a while a focus on another matter. You have to weigh the cost of what it will take to get back that material or ground. For example, in trial you may seek to be more likeable than your opponent in front of the jury. At some point you may want to shed that persona so that you can strike at a witness and hurt them beyond repair in such a way that is worth it to your case. If you then want to come back into likable mode, that may be a position impossible to recover completely, and a cost determination in abandoning it must be made, i.e. how much will you lose of your likeability to deliver a severe blow to a witness by being harsh? Say, with a sympathetic witness for the other side such as a victim, whose credibility must be destroyed beyond all repair.

5. From a position of this sort, if the enemy is unprepared, you may sally forth and defeat him. But if the enemy is prepared for your coming, and you fail to defeat him, then, return being impossible, disaster will ensue.

Taking the above example, it may not be just that you lose some likability but that you fall so far that you can't gain it back, and the other lawyer is given the opening to try to be more of the likable lawyer. It seems like a grade-school level concept but so many jurors function at relatively low levels, and they are often confused by legal concepts or propositions put forth by expert witnesses. As such, although they hate to admit it, they will directly or subconsciously start to favor the side they simply like better. This is a point that has been proven time after time over the years.[6]

6. When the position is such that neither side will gain by making the first move, it is called temporizing ground.

7. In a position of this sort, even though the enemy should offer us an attractive bait, it will be advisable not to stir forth, but rather to retreat, thus enticing the enemy in his turn; then, when part of his army has come out, we may deliver our attack with advantage.

Sometimes it can be wise to entice an opponent to take the bait to weaken their position. For example, it can be beneficial to get an opponent lawyer who is trying to seem more likable to get baited into an argument with one of your lawyers or witnesses that makes them go out of character. It can be impossible for them to try to take up a position of the nicer or more likable lawyer after they have made slights in front of the jury that leave a bad impression on the jury. You will also want to bait a key opponent witness into losing their cool or some other error that they can't escape.

8. With regard to narrow passes, if you can occupy them first, let them be strongly garrisoned and await the advent of the enemy.

Getting an opponent bottled into a strategy where they must travel down a certain path with no real ways to deviate has numerous benefits. Once you have them locked in, you can wait at a key bottleneck and deliver a blow. Going back to the DUI example; if you have a great attack for a breath test result then

---

[6] *What Makes Juries Listen Today* by Sonya Hamlin (Thomson Legal Works, 1998).

get the state committed to it in front of the jury as their best argument. If you can do that, then successfully attack that point, it will seem that they are falling back on just the field tests as enough proof which will fly in the face of their earlier touting of the breath test result. I once had an OWI case where the test was above the margin of error above the legal limit but when I showed up for trial, I saw that the state had to switch their state expert. I knew him from when I was a prosecutor, and I knew that he would give me more than the others would, as far as the open container in the car being enough to get him below the level when driving. The state did not know that, so they leaned heavily on the breath test result in opening but then had to rest mostly on the field tests in closings. The jury was hung six-six, and the state elected to not re-try the case.

9. Should the army forestall you in occupying a pass, do not go after him if the pass is fully garrisoned, but only if it is weakly garrisoned.

Conversely, if at all possible, you must keep aware of how your opponent is situated, so that you do not approach an issue at a point when they are poised to fight you more easily on it. Of course, this sentence basically says: don't walk into your opponent's trap. Obviously, this is not a revolutionary concept. It is also easy to state here. The reason why it bears mentioning is because you have to be aware of where possible stumbles can occur for you or your witnesses. Only *you* can properly review the case to see where there are points where you will likely have to take a hit. It may be material you can't ignore all together, so you must look at the best way to approach it. You should also prep your expert and lay witnesses so they may be prepared to take hits and be ready to deal with them. You can't avoid ever taking a hit, but you can do what you can to be aware of when and where it will come, as well as how best to take the hit so that its impact is minimal.

10. With regard to precipitous heights, if you are beforehand with your adversary, you should occupy the raised and sunny spots, and there wait for him to come up.

The high ground has been a strategic concept since the beginning of time, and it is one that's a familiar rule to those not even familiar with strategy. There is a reason that it is so well known and that is because it contains such a universal truth: you want to hold the heights on any battlefield as those positions control the ground around it. In war that was due to the use of arrows and artillery, but the geographical advantages of those spots were significant, given the fundamental rule that, if an army is to charge uphill, it will exert more than an army that runs downhill. Also, arrows, artillery, and bullets from rifles can travel further as the ground slopes down than they can uphill.

Key evidence and positions such as an expert should be considered high ground in court. There are cases where one side will have an expert and one will not, such as a DUI case where the state has a lab tech or better expert to talk about validity of the testing procedures for a body sample. In such cases the defense has to go uphill to attack. Of course, the mere presence of high ground will not guarantee a win but rarely in such a case can you simply ignore the high-ground positions and seek to win the day without making a challenge of this position. There is also something to be said for trying to get to these points first in front of the jury. The natural progression of a case is that the plaintiff will get the chance to present an opening first. Some jurisdictions allow the defense to defer opening to the start of their case, but I have never seen that as a good tactic. Although it may be painful to have the jury sit through the plaintiff's opening and allow them to hear points unchecked, you can and should argue as much as you can get away with in opening on those points to leave them with doubts as they listen to the plaintiff witnesses. Even before this, however, you must try to raise points of argument and concern in jury selection.

Many lawyers who will freely object in trial will not do so in jury selection. Until the jury is empaneled, there is little risk of a mistrial that will not allow for a new trial. Even if you can't get into as many facts of the case, the ultimate high ground in a criminal case is reasonable doubt. The defense should be the first one there and try to occupy it by using that sacred defense tool to empower your client's case. The concept of 'beyond a reasonable doubt' should be a significant point of your jury selection objectives. Getting to these key points early can be key in your later success during the trial. Regardless of the law, you can't presume the jury will follow its duty to wait until the end of the trial to make decisions.

Tactically speaking there are natural heights in the courtroom. The judge, of course, occupies literal high ground to give them more natural prestige and presence, but there are favorable places a lawyer can move to. When directing a witness, you want to stand close to the jury, so the witness naturally looks toward the jury. The eye contact from the witness to the jury will help even a nervous witness seem naturally more credible to the jury, as studies have shown. Conversely, standing further away from the jury, to keep the witness eye contact down during a cross examination of your opponents' witness, is preferred.[7]

11. If the enemy has occupied them before you, do not follow him, but retreat and try to entice him away.

If your opponent has made a solid position on a key point or area of dispute, such as with an expert, it may be wiser to not try to take on the expert themselves at the zenith of their strength but to use subsequent witnesses to dispute the expert's reasoning or to simply triage the case until your expert comes to testify and discredit the

---

[7] *What Makes Juries Listen Today* by Sonya Hamlin (Thomson Legal Works, 1998).

opponent's earlier expert witness. This can be dangerous, but it is better than going on a long cross of the opponent expert that does nothing to them but possibly bolster their credibility even further.

12. If you are situated at a great distance from the enemy, and the strength of the two armies is equal, it is not easy to provoke a battle, and fighting will be to your disadvantage.

Conversely, your opponent may not seek to duke it out with your expert. Although it is nice for them to have material to bring out on cross, don't count on it happening and make sure all *needed* material comes out on direct.

13. These six are the principles connected with Earth. The general who has attained a responsible post must be careful to study them.

14. Now an army is exposed to six several calamities, not arising from natural causes, but from faults for which the general is responsible. These are: (1) Flight; (2) insubordination; (3) collapse; (4) ruin; (5) disorganization; (6) rout.

In the end if you lose, it is your fault. One can point to bad luck or a crazy renegade juror but those things happen and, in the end, both in reality and certainly in the eyes of your client, the buck stops with you.

15. Other conditions being equal, if one force is hurled against another ten times its size, the result will be the flight of the former.

If your position is truly unalterably weaker than your opponent, then don't fight an unwinnable battle. Most cases will settle. A very small number of cases actually go to trial, and mostly those go to trial as they are close enough to have a fighting issue. If, before trial or even during, you see things proceeding unfavorably, then take a deal. You will, of course, need to manage expectations and prepare a client for such a reality ahead of time. After they have seen a powerful opening from your opponent or the makeup of the jury after jury selection, they may decide that a settlement is better than a total loss after all. If you are forced into trial with no viable argument, then you must be sure you have done all you can to avoid an appeal based on your deficiency. In the end those may be some of your most favorite trials, as you have little to lose and are forced into very creative tactics.

16. When the common soldiers are too strong and their officers too weak, the result is insubordination. When the officers are too strong and the common soldiers too weak, the result is collapse.

Not everyone on the team may be an all-star, and there may be an MVP in a big win, but the practice of law should still be seen as a team sport, so to speak. The best lawyer will still need good and clearly presented evidence as well as good witnesses to help support those facts. They will need presentations of and organization of evidence in complex litigation that even with technology can rarely be done on their own. That being said a dictatorship will run more smoothly than a democracy. There must be a clear vision. A commander can certainly listen to his top lieutenants but in the end the choice is with the one true leader. If their directives are not followed, then the subordinates may throw the plan off intentionally or unintentionally. If the team is incapable of executing their parts, then the best of lawyers can't carry the whole day without the support work of other lawyers or staff on the team.

We live in an age where we grow up thinking we can be the most famous athlete or the biggest rock star. As a team leader you will encounter much more vainglorious lawyers on your team. You have to confront this issue from the get-go and make sure there are no stars who seek to be more important than the team and client goals.

17. When the higher officers are angry and insubordinate, and on meeting the enemy give battle on their own account from a feeling of resentment, before the commander-in-chief can tell whether he is in a position to fight, the result is ruin.

You have to maintain enough discipline to make sure that a lawyer doesn't go off-plan at a deposition or trial, whether it be deliberate or in the heat of the moment. The plan must be known and clear to all, so if there are sidetracks then you will know if it is due to insubordination or a necessary audible.

18. When the general is weak and without authority; when his orders are not clear and distinct; when there are no fixes, duties assigned to officers and men, and the ranks are formed in a slovenly haphazard manner, the result is utter disorganization.

You must strike a balance of discipline without inspiring discord in your team. Your team must take care to handle their tasks with great care. They may not know where it fits into the plan overall or they may not be as enthusiastic about the plan as you, but you must make sure they still follow the plan and do their part accordingly.

19. When a general, unable to estimate the enemy's strength, allows an inferior force to engage a larger one, or hurls a weak detachment against a powerful one, and neglects to place picked soldiers in the front rank, the result must be rout.

You must pick your team members for tasks based on their abilities without making it too obvious that you do or don't have faith in certain members to do more critical tasks. You must evaluate the strengths and weaknesses of your team without consideration of their feelings or who you like and don't like as much. They should also understand, if they are professionals, that it is not personal but rather for the good of the team and the client that your choices are made. If you choose a weaker member to face an opponent team member who uses their ability to gain an advantage, then the fault is with you more than the team member.

I have always struggled with jury selection. I show up for a trial on day one wanting to rip an opponent's head off. Yet aside from any last minute pre-trial hearing matters, you start with jury section. It is critical that you come out of jury selection with your likeability improved or at least intact, and that is not always easy to do when you are pumped up and ready for a fight. Imagine a boxer who walks out into the ring and has to spend a half hour reading children's stories to grade school kids before the fight can get started. Although there are key strategic goals to accomplish in jury selection, you certainly can't be argumentative with the jurors themselves if one gives you an answer to a question that is not to your benefit. Because I know this about myself, I always am willing to get help in jury selection or simply have the most personable member of the team complete that part of the case. You have to know strengths and weaknesses. You can't be the greatest at everything, so the only strategic choice is to recognize those flaws and put the best people in the driver's seat for the parts of the case they are suited for.

20. These are six ways of courting defeat, which must be carefully noted by the general who has attained a responsible post.

Don't let ego or poor judgment cost you and your client a win.

21. The natural formation of the country is the soldier's best ally; but a power of estimating the adversary, of controlling the forces of victory, and of shrewdly calculating difficulties, dangers and distances, constitutes the test of a great general.

If you are honest with yourself in analyzing a loss, you will see the bulk of the fault lies with your decisions and not those of your team. Your decisions are not made in a vacuum. You must not be negatively impacted in your calculations by ego, vanity, emotion, or anything else that may cloud your judgement.

22. He who knows these things, and in fighting puts his knowledge into practice, will win his battles. He who knows them not, nor practices them, will surely be defeated.

If you take your eyes of the road ahead for even a moment at even the most benign deposition or hearing, then you can cost you and your client dearly.

23. If fighting is sure to result in victory, then you must fight, even though the ruler forbids it; if fighting will not result in victory, then you must not fight even at the ruler's bidding.

You will know better than your client whether you can win a battle or not. The client gets to choose, as would the leader of the state. Your rules of ethics for your jurisdiction will almost certainly require that they make final decisions. Don't be afraid to bombard the client with CYA letters or emails and to even make a record of last offers, etc. to bolster any future complaints after a loss that the client insisted on against your advice. Just as a general is responsible to the state, you must paint your client the whole picture, so they can make a proper decision. They will let their emotions affect them, but it is your job to make sure they can understand their position as much as they are able to.

24. The general who advances without coveting fame and retreats without fearing disgrace, whose only thought is to protect his country and do good service for his sovereign, is the jewel of the kingdom.

You are only as good a lawyer as you keep your oath to your clients and yourself. You must not worry about what your colleagues will or won't think of you. You can't make decisions based on press coverage, no matter how much you think it may get you future clients and fame. For example, if it is best for your client to avoid more press attention, then use your connections to get your client brought in via a side door, etc.

25. Regard your soldiers as your children, and they will follow you into the deepest valleys; look upon them as your own beloved sons, and they will stand by you even unto death.

In war their lives may be on the line. In law they are not, but all young layers do crave something deeply, and that is knowledge. You can promise to teach them how things really work and give them the tools to be a good lawyer themselves. Law school only does so much. Most successful lawyers of renown refer to experience as to why they have the skills and careers that they do. The best life lessons are those delivered to us like a kick in the groin. Helping your young team members learn those lessons *without* the pain will be cherished by intelligent young lawyers. Most younger lawyers will refer to what they learned in internships or through legal clinics. etc. as being of more value to them on day one of being a lawyer than what they learned from textbooks.

26. If, however, you are indulgent, but unable to make your authority felt; kind-hearted, but unable to enforce your commands; and incapable, moreover, of quelling disorder: then your soldiers must be likened to spoilt children; they are useless for any practical purpose.

Internal cliques or divisions among your team can be deadly to the team's chemistry. You will want them to go out for a beer and bond, adding on the team's strength, but jealousy or internal romances and distractions can be deadly to the team as a whole.

27. If we know that our own men are in a condition to attack but are unaware that the enemy is not open to attack, we have gone only halfway towards victory.

Your opponent will likely go out to bond, etc. You can learn about their camaraderie as a window into their team strength. You may know exactly what your team's morale is or their individual strengths, but you may take steps to learn the same about your opponent. Even if you are only facing one lawyer on the other side, you can still find out about them as well. A prosecutor with a heavy case load or a lawyer who is having marital problems, etc. can give you some idea about their ability to focus and stay on the task at hand. It will never serve as a reason for you to take your foot off the gas, but it can still be good to know.

28. If we know that the enemy is open to attack but are unaware that our own men are not in a condition to attack, we have gone only halfway towards victory.

It is far easier to keep up on your team's morale and ability. To not take note of such things is inexcusable as it is literally right in front of you.

29. If we know that the enemy is open to attack, and also know that our men are in a condition to attack but are unaware that the nature of the ground makes fighting impracticable, we have still gone only halfway towards victory.

It is more than just you and them. The jury makeup will be a factor. The climate in the community is a factor. For example, if there is a high-profile domestic assault murder case such as with Oscar Pistorius, then you know that will be on the mind of your potential jurors in a misdemeanor domestic assault case, or if a recent DUI fatality case is in the news, then that will affect your standard DUI case. The judge assigned to a case is a factor. If your client is a minority and the local populace is predominantly white, that is a factor. There are numerous factors to be considered and although the strengths of the legal teams are big factors, they are only part of the overall equation that leads to one verdict or another.

30. Hence the experienced soldier, once in motion, is never bewildered; once he has broken camp, he is never at a loss.

Presuming that you move *only* after considering all relevant materials, and you use your experience and wisdom to make the decisions, then you will put yourself and your client in the best possible position to win.

31. Hence the saying: If you know the enemy and know yourself, your victory will not stand in doubt; if you know Heaven and know Earth, you may make your victory complete.

XI. The Nine Situations

1. Sun Tzu said: The art of war recognizes nine varieties of ground: (1) Dispersive ground; (2) facile ground; (3) contentious ground; (4) open ground; (5) ground of intersecting highways; (6) serious ground; (7) difficult ground; (8) hemmed-in ground; (9) desperate ground.

2. When a chieftain is fighting in his own territory, it is dispersive ground.

Getting 'home-teamed' is a commonly referred to term in the law for a reason. When you are fighting a case far from your home jurisdiction, you must wonder if the local lawyer has ties to the clerk and court that will offer advantages to them that you don't have. The local lawyer may have favorable reputation with the local jury pool as well. There are nearly countless advantages to be a local lawyer opposing an out-of-towner. Should this be true? No. Is it true? Yes.

Sometimes there is a benefit to being the out-of-towner, say on a criminal case. If you have a client with one prosecutor, and you are almost never in that county or jurisdiction, then you won't worry much about what is to happen if they grow to hate you. If you anger a prosecutor, you see often on one case, then you may be concerned on how they will treat you on other cases, when you are more at their mercy, as those cases are not as strong for you.

Another way to interpret this section is to think of dispersive ground as material you are familiar with. If you are a very successful DUI lawyer and that is the majority of your practice, then you may feel out of sorts when taking on a sex abuse or other kind of criminal matter. There are often nuances in the law that are limited to a particular type of crime that won't be familiar to you if you hardly ever take clients on those cases. Conversely, if you take an out-of-town sex-abuse case in a small jurisdiction which doesn't handle many of those types of cases, and you do, then you will have a clear advantage over the opponent.

3. When he has penetrated into hostile territory, but to no great distance, it is facile ground.

You can still pull back and are never so far along a course that you can't possibly change course on your plan if new information comes to light. You may find yourself at depositions with no best way forward yet mapped, and you have to truly learn the opponent's evidence before you can commit to a particular choice of argument on a case. You don't want to commit to a plan and not be able to still look for a better one, based on material that becomes available to you.

4. Ground the possession of which imports great advantage to either side, is contentious ground.

These are positions worth fighting for because, if your enemy gets them, it will give them advantages to win the whole case. The fight over the key expert witness fact is an example of this. In a case where dueling experts offer contradictory material to the jury, you will want to fight to support your expert and tear down theirs as it can be the key to swaying the jury one way or another. A fight over the validity and manner of taking a body sample for testing to be used for DNA or an alcohol measurement, etc. is going to be beyond critical in a criminal case. If one side takes an advantage on such a topic, the whole case can go one way or the other based on who holds sway with the jury on this single point.

5. Ground on which each side has liberty of movement is open ground.

This can be material in a case where each side can take the position and gain advantage but yet also you can move on from it without great concern. Examples of such material would be things that you both can lay claim to, such as the moral right, or you are both seeking justice for your client.

6. Ground which forms the key to three contiguous states, so that he who occupies it first has most of the Empire at his command, is a ground of intersecting highways.

Some points are only worth taking if they control the path to another more critical piece of evidence. One witness, such as a foundational witness, may not seem to the jury, correctly, as key, but they must be handled with care if they will open the door to more critical witness testimony later. For example, when an expert witness is to offer DNA or bodily samples, then that witness can only proceed with their key testimony if it first shown that the sample was delivered to the lab correctly and a chain of custody has been maintained.

7. When an army has penetrated into the heart of a hostile country, leaving a number of fortified cities in its rear, it is serious ground.

Once you are forward and entrenched in an argument, it is very hard to pull back on it. Especially in the trial, you can't diverge too far from what you promised in opening. For example, if you make points in opening that an expert will be critical about later, it will be nearly impossible to completely downplay that expert, whether it be one of yours that fell apart or one of theirs that held strong.

8. Mountain forests, rugged steeps, marshes and fens—all country that is hard to traverse: this is difficult ground.

For the jury to still be following you, complex ground can be hard to traverse. You have to explain complex topics while maintaining their complexity for the record and still having it come out in such a way that a juror, who is completely unfamiliar with the topic and of average intelligence, can still grasp it. This must be done without alienating the jury or making them feel inferior. You don't want them to hate you, and they may never truly understand the material, but rather they may vote on the expert they feel is simply more credible in their opinion. It is not uncommon in exit polling for a juror to say they didn't understand key points but that they feel strongly one expert was more believable then the other.

9. Ground, which is reached through narrow gorges, and from which we can only retire by tortuous paths, so that a small number of the enemy would suffice to crush a large body of our men: this is hemmed in ground.

Some paths you may want to take because the gain is tempting, yet if you do, you can be stuck in a place that will offer an easy ambush or counterattack from better positions. Such risks-versus-reward analysis will need to be done on a case-by-case basis.

10. Ground on which we can only be saved from destruction by fighting without delay, is desperate ground.

Such ground in a criminal case is material you must have but it is dangerous. You need to get the point and get out. Don't dwell too long with an expert if you feel you have gotten what you needed or what was possible. If you continue with them, they might gain back some or all of the ground you had picked up. In most jurisdictions if they are rehabilitated too well, you can still re-cross them again, but generally your chances get worse on re-cross. Also, you may have to make decisions in such fights without the benefit of time to analyze them. If you did not anticipate being in this area at trial, you will need to make very quick decisions that you may come to regret.

11. On dispersive ground, therefore, fight not. On facile ground, halt not. On contentious ground, attack not.

12. On open ground, do not try to block the enemy's way. On the ground of intersecting highways, join hands with your allies.

13. On serious ground, gather in plunder. In difficult ground, keep steadily on the march.

14. On hemmed-in ground, resort to stratagem. On desperate ground, fight.

15. Those who were called skillful leaders of old knew how to drive a wedge between the enemy's front and rear; to prevent co-operation between his large and small divisions; to hinder the good troops from rescuing the bad, the officers from rallying their men.

You don't have to wait for an opponent to get up to start boxing again. This is a contest with rules, but there is no rule against hitting someone when they are down in this contest. You don't have to give them time to get up or a standing-eight count before you strike again. There is professionalism but you owe it to the client to press home an advantage. Litigation has rules but being lady-like or gentlemanly is not the way forward. As long as you don't make the jury dislike you and you are within the rules, then *do it*.

16. When the enemy's men were united, they managed to keep them in disorder.

Do what you can to keep your opponent on the back foot. This often will come from decisions you make at the time and not part of your initial plans. If you have a chance to disrupt your opponent without negatively affecting your plans, do so. There are many ways to do this but the most obvious one is to object, i.e. to throw your opponent off rhythm during a time when they are advancing a key point. You can also ask for a recess as long as it doesn't look like you are trying to circle the wagons or are caught off guard yourself. Approach the bench and ask for an early lunch (when lunch is close) or some other option if you want to slow them down when they are on a roll.

17. When it was to their advantage, they made a forward move; when otherwise, they stopped still.

There are often reasons as to why your opponent is making a choice or doing what they are doing. You have to be aware of the 'whys?' behind their actions and consider the clues you notice to tell you how you should act.

18. If asked how to cope with a great host of the enemy in orderly array and on the point of marching to the attack, I should say: "Begin by seizing something which your opponent holds dear; then he will be amenable to your will."

You can control the tone in a trial. If you can get your opponent to constantly address topics you raise, then you can set the tone and course of the proceedings. This is often easier for a plaintiff or prosecutor, as the jury hears from them so much more in the initial stages. The defense opening and cross examinations are your time to raise other issues to get the jury thinking about your theories of the case. Juries are required to wait to make their decisions until they hear everything, but that simply is not how most people function, and you can't wait until it is your turn to get them on board with your theory of the case.

19. Rapidity is the essence of war: take advantage of the enemy's unreadiness, make your way by unexpected routes, and attack unguarded spots.

Deception and stealth are key in war. In litigation there are rules for discovery and disclosure, but you should still hold your cards close on a tactical level, so that the opponent is not sure of what you are planning to do until the last minute. Every trial will have at least one opportunity to surprise your opponent. There will be little to lose in such moments and a lot to gain.

20. The following are the principles to be observed by an invading force: The further you penetrate into a country, the greater will be the solidarity of your troops, and thus the defenders will not prevail against you.

The farther in you go into the case, you likely reach points of no return where the client and your team may feel that you are committed absolutely to the cause. Many resolutions to cases have been made while in trial, and if the case warrants it, it should not be ignored. However, when you reject an offer from the state in a criminal case or an amount in a civil case, then, certainly, you should feel you are so far in, especially on a case that has been pending months or years, that it should have the effect of a milestone or event that bears substantial consideration. You can't let your ego or your desire to win get in the way of a realistic last-minute or mid-trial offer if it is a good one for the client to take. You should record during trial any offers that your client has refused to accept.

21. Make forays in fertile country in order to supply your army with food.

Don't interpret this to mean that you should steal your opponent's legal pads and post-its off of their table at court or during a deposition, of course, but rather keep in mind ways you plan to score points or even get a key part of your closing from their witnesses. Nothing stings more than using a foul-up by their lawyer or witness against them in closing. They can lead to some of the most powerful and substantial things that sticks with the jurors. To say "even their expert that they paid to be here had to agree with me about…" can really hit home with the jury.

22. Carefully study the well-being of your men, and do not overtax them. Concentrate your energy and hoard your strength. Keep your army continually on the move and devise unfathomable plans.

Keeping your team of lawyers and witnesses on the same page can be difficult. Once things shift during the trial, you have to be mindful of witness-sequestration rules and make sure they are not talking to each other about the case, while at the same time you may want to carefully advise a witness, before they take the stand, what is going on if the ground has shifted beneath them. Carefully study your jurisdiction's rules on this because you don't want to draw a bar complaint or let a witness get thrown off as they don't know what has changed. Don't be afraid to ask for a recess to talk to a witness, as you may be able to at the last minute.

23. Throw your soldiers into positions whence there is no escape, and they will prefer death to flight. If they will face death, there is nothing they may not achieve. Officers and men alike will put forth their uttermost strength.

But for a death penalty case for your client, this will not be the case. However, if the firm that the associates want to be partners in will go bankrupt without a win in a civil suit or if the team members fear being fired from the firm, then they will be motivated. If they have been promised bonuses based only on victory, they will take it upon themselves to spend extra time and efforts on the client's and firm's behalf.

24. Soldiers when in desperate straits lose the sense of fear. If there is no place of refuge, they will stand firm. If they are in hostile country, they will show a stubborn front. If there is no help for it, they will fight hard.

Fear of losing something that is desired has always been the best motivator of men and women.

25. Thus, without waiting to be marshaled, the soldiers will be constantly on the qui vive; without waiting to be asked, they will do your will; without restrictions, they will be faithful; without giving orders, they can be trusted.

If you find what motivates your individual team members, then you will be able to get the most out of them every day.

26. Prohibit the taking of omens and do away with superstitious doubts. Then, until death itself comes, no calamity need be feared.

Just like in war and even among professional athletes, your team members will look at omens and other events as a sign of future success. When any person has so much at stake, their fear will push toward considerations not completely based on logic but rather based on emotional thoughts or feelings. You must do what you can to make sure they don't yield to such signs or concerns, so they do not get distracted or psyched themselves out at the wrong time.

27. If our soldiers are not overburdened with money, it is not because they have a distaste for riches; if their lives are not unduly long, it is not because they are disinclined to longevity.

There can be members of your team that truly are there for the fight. Although they may like money and even spend it lavishly, some of the best members of the team will be those that truly enjoy the fight, enjoy the contest. There are only a few occupations where winning and losing are so brightly defined and sought after. A successful large corporation may grow by a set goal and their stock may be affected based on if they reach that goal; it is still not the same as pure and absolute winning or losing. You can have some civil suits where you win but are not awarded as much as you thought was obtainable from the jury. A doctor may have a patient that dies or one where a surgery does not fix the ailment as they thought it would. However, to hear a jury say guilty or not guilty or an appellate court overturn or affirm a lower court is a rare absolute. The thrill of the hunt or the buzz of combat is something that some lawyers need. That is a wonderful character trait for your team members to have.

28. On the day they are ordered out to battle, your soldiers may weep, those sitting up bedewing their garments, and those lying down letting the tears run down their cheeks. But let them once be brought to bay, and they will display the courage of a Chu or a Kuei.

It is ok to be nervous. Fear is a natural and powerful motivator. I can't recall an appellate hearing or trial where I didn't have at least some anxiety. I always have habits such as eating very small meals for lunch and breakfast on contested court dates, as I feal it helps me maximize my sharpness. Experience certainly makes contested hearings and proceedings easier or more natural. Whatever you call it, if you feel nothing on the morning of a big court date, then you are probably not doing your best possible work for the client. You should feel in your gut a tension or tightness before any big hearing. It simply means you are vested in the case. Whether you like or don't like your client, you should still feel a passion to win, to champion the argument that it is your duty to present. If you don't, are you truly fulfilling your oath? Some lawyers have great passion for certain issues or clients, but you should always draw your passion from your commitment to the fight, regardless of what you are fighting about.

29. The skillful tactician may be likened to the shuai-jan. Now the shuai-jan is a snake that is found in the Chung mountains.

Strike at its head, and you will be attacked by its tail; strike at its tail, and you will be attacked by its head; strike at its middle, and you will be attacked by head and tail both.

Your abilities combined with extreme preparation will enable you to adjust with almost Zen-like unconscious or instinctive response to attacks at any point. A general rule of thumb is that you should prepare eight hours for every hour of trial at a minimum.

30. Asked if an army can be made to imitate the shuai-jan, I should answer, yes. For the men of Wu and the men of Yueh are enemies; yet if they are crossing a river in the same boat and are caught by a storm, they will come to each other's assistance just as the left hand helps the right.

Your team should not be willing to let a team member fail to look better than themselves or curry more favor from you if it means the case itself will suffer. No matter how much the members may want to obtain the riches your firm has to offer, they should not be willing to step over the other members at the cost of losing even a part of the strength of the case. They should be helping each other, and if they don't, they should not be on your team. No one should be above the team and its goals.

31. Hence it is not enough to put one's trust in the tethering of horses, and the burying of chariot wheels in the ground

Things will go wrong. The best of plans will develop flaws. You should certainly not waste time for blame at trial but rather focus 100% of your efforts on fixing a problem. There will be plenty of time to take a deep dive into why something went wrong after the trial is over.

32. The principle on which to manage an army is to set up one standard of courage which all must reach.

Pausing or hesitating to help another team member at a time of need due to personal goals or feelings toward a team member should never exist in the team. It can be poison to those in the foxhole together who must be able to trust each other at critical moments.

33. How to make the best of both strong and weak—that is a question involving the proper use of ground.

After working up the case you should grow to know the strengths and weakness of each member long before trial, even if it is your first case with them. No matter your ability as a lawyer, you will need to master this skill to lead your team of lawyers on a case.

34. Thus the skillful general conducts his army just as though he were leading a single man, by the hand.

You have to keep the team on the same page and going in the same direction at all times, both your lawyers and the witnesses, as much as the rules allow.

35. It is the business of a general to be quiet and thus ensure secrecy; upright and just, and thus maintain order.

Giles translates this section as above. Griffith offers "It is the business of a General to be serene and inscrutable, impartial, and self-controlled." This seems to fit in with the rest of the book much clearer. Leaders do not need to yell or have emotional outbursts at their team. Poise and control will generate more respect and belief in the team especially when they may not be sure of the plan.

36. He must be able to mystify his officers and men by false reports and appearances, and thus keep them in total ignorance.

Again, if you have control over the team, there is no reason to hide things from them. They may even see something you have missed. In the end, the leader of the team must be the one to choose the path forward.

37. By altering his arrangements and changing his plans, he keeps the enemy without definite knowledge. By shifting his camp and taking circuitous routes, he prevents the enemy from anticipating his purpose.

You want the enemy not to be able to predict exactly how you will come at them or each witness in turn, etc. During the course of litigation, you may need to highlight a point or weakness of a witness to seek a favorable plea offer from the other side. This issue may reveal how you plan to attack that same flaw at trial. You must do what you can to present the flaw to the opponent in a way that doesn't affect your ability to still use it at trial. Altering it in some way or attacking it through a new method will be key, without reducing its strength.

38. At the critical moment, the leader of an army acts like one who has climbed up a height and then kicks away the ladder behind him. He carries his men deep into hostile territory before he shows his hand.

If possible, you want the team to be onboard with your plans. At some point, because you are the one making decisions, as a leader of the team you have to make the call, and if possible, make it so there is no way to back out now. Once you commit the case to a certain path, then it is easier to keep the team onboard with the plan, as they should see that there can be no change now.

39. He burns his boats and breaks his cooking-pots; like a shepherd driving a flock of sheep, he drives his men this way and that, and nothing knows whither he is going.

If you are confident in your plan or approach, there are ways to lock your team into it. This can be beneficial to prevent wasting time when entertaining alternatives from your team. I generally appreciate the thoughts of my team with a fresh pair of eyes. In the end there will be usually just one way to go forward. There is no scientific test to say which is the best way, as our profession is afforded no such luxury; there is just your professional opinion, and even then, when you really are right and no lawyer would have done it differently from you, an oddball jury may go against what they should have done.

40. To muster his host and bring it into danger:—this may be termed the business of the general.

Getting the opponent in a position that you choose to attack him from is far better than simply waiting and hoping for them to go there. You can use opening to call out an issue that you want the other side to address or bring up key points with witnesses on cross, etc. In a DUI test case you may want to call out in opening that there are issues with how the sample was collected, etc. to force the state to deal with it early on, if that will be beneficial to you.

41. The different measures suited to the nine varieties of ground; the expediency of aggressive or defensive tactics; and the fundamental laws of human nature: these are things that must most certainly be studied.

42. When invading hostile territory, the general principle is, that penetrating deeply brings cohesion; penetrating but a short way means dispersion.

When you get deeper into the heart of the opponent's case, your team needs to stay focused on the primary attack points and not be distracted by attractive diversions.

43. When you leave your own country behind, and take your army across neighborhood territory, you find yourself on critical ground. When there are means of communication on all four sides, the ground is one of intersecting highways.

Nothing can hurt your team more or faster than a team that is not communicating with each other. During parts of the case, you will literally be in the same room and can communicate as needed.

At other times you can be miles away, but you must be available to them at any moment. Current technology offers countless communication tools that were not previously available only a few short years ago. Take advantage of them.

44. When you penetrate deeply into a country, it is serious ground. When you penetrate but a little way, it is facile ground.

It would be beyond fascinating to hear what Sun Tzu would say in light of current communication options available to even a poor army. The ability to talk or send complete pages of notes and video conferences would certainly have led to greater expectations for communication and perhaps for direct involvement with the team leader in every corner of the battlefield.

45. When you have the enemy's strongholds on your rear, and narrow passes in front, it is hemmed-in ground. When there is no place of refuge at all, it is desperate ground.

Once in trial and facing the fight in the moment, your options for changing key material or strategies will be limited. Additionally, once you pass deadlines, such as for discovery, then there also may be limited options for shifting, if needed. Plan ahead as much as possible and make contingency plans for possible shifts you believe might occur. There will always be some 'fog of war' as you must presume that, just as you have done, the other side will endeavor to keep their cards close on a tactical issue that they hold in reserve for trial to catch you out with. Much of your planning has to be focused on studying the opponent's situation to predict what they will do to you.

46. Therefore, on dispersive ground, I would inspire my men with unity of purpose. On facile ground, I would see that there is close connection between all parts of my army.

47. On contentious ground, I would hurry up my rear.

When the fight is well and truly at hand, then you need to keep your resources all close and keep your team tight. Make sure you have all you need at court. Don't worry about leaving a member in the office to take new client calls if you think there may be a reason to have them with you at court.

48. On open ground, I would keep a vigilant eye on my defenses. On ground of intersecting highways, I would consolidate my alliances.

49. On serious ground, I would try to ensure a continuous stream of supplies. On difficult ground, I would keep pushing on along the road.

You have to make careful decisions. When your witness is done with their testimony, they will want to leave. Can you allow them to or is there a chance they will need to be recalled? If you do let them leave, will the judge allow you a delay to get them back? It is important to know what remedies you may have open to you if you need to recall them or get a delay of some kind. Knowing the judge and local rules or customs are key to this as well.

If you are presenting a key point, you want it to come in as cleanly as possible, so there is little doubt about its validity. Don't waver or wonder off on a tangent or switch topics and hope things are still clear when you come back to the key issue with a witness. Keep in mind that the jury has not spent the time you have to become familiar with the material. You have to bring in the important material down a clear path so the jurors can follow it, and make sure that the material comes in clearly and smoothly.

50. On hemmed-in ground, I would block any way of retreat. On desperate ground, I would proclaim to my soldiers the hopelessness of saving their lives.

When Hernán Cortés arrived in the new world in 1519, he encountered resistance from his own people because they were tired and not motivated, so he literally burned his ships.[8] This is now a term for motiving your people by making them aware that there is no way to go back and change things; so you have to put all your effort into what we are doing here if you want to make it. If your team is made up of smart people that you have chosen, then by all means, listen to them and be open to what they have to say, but at some point there will be a time for you to say that we are now fully committed to a certain way forward.

51. For it is the soldier's disposition to offer an obstinate resistance when surrounded, to fight hard when he cannot help himself, and to obey promptly when he has fallen into danger.

Once your team knows that there is no other way, then they should be motivated to go with you on the way that is set out, and do their best to help make it the right way to have gone.

52. We cannot enter into alliance with neighboring princes until we are acquainted with their designs. We are not fit to lead an army on the march unless we are familiar with the face of the country—its mountains and forests, its pitfalls and precipices, its marshes and swamps. We shall be unable to turn natural advantages to account unless we make use of local guides.

In some cases there will be criminal co-defendants and others participating in a suit against a common target. Great analysis must be taken to decide if they should be your allies or not. Conversely, a criminal prosecutor may try to get one defendant to place blame on another and turn against them for their own interests.

---

[8] John Pemberton, *Conquistadors: Searching for El Dorado: The Terrifying Spanish Conquest of the Aztec and Inca Empires* (Futura, London: 2011).

There is also a danger that the lawyer for a co-defendant, etc. may not be a good one. If the matter proceeds to trial, there is a danger that they may make a mistake that makes all the defendants look more guilty, etc. You must find out all you can on your ally's lawyer. As noted earlier, you also have to learn about the local rules and proclivities of your judge to be sure exactly what the lay of the land truly is. You can never say your calculations are good unless you know all you can about every variable.

53. To be ignored of any one of the following four or five principles does not befit a warlike prince.

54. When a warlike prince attacks a powerful state, his generalship shows itself in preventing the concentration of the enemy's forces. He overawes his opponents, and their allies are prevented from joining against him.

Keeping your opponent's witnesses off the same page is difficult. Once you learn of the other side's planned order of witnesses, it can be far easier to cause derision and even getting the opponent to have to recall a previous witness for clarification, and lead the jury to infer that the opponent's argument is unstable. Making a point with a witness that can only truly be rebutted by a witness that has already been called can lead to the recall and breaks your opponent's flow. Conversely, if your opponent does that to you, then you must seem as if nothing is amiss, and all is planned. Often the jury doesn't know something is going against your intent until your words, or expressions, unintendedly tells them so.

55. Hence he does not strive to ally himself with all and sundry, nor does he foster the power of other states. He carries out his own secret designs, keeping his antagonists in awe. Thus, he is able to capture their cities and overthrow their kingdoms.

If you decide to take allies, then you must closely regulate what you or your team offers. Also, by surprise, if you can get an opponent witness out of sorts, then they seem much less effective even on points that they should carry in their favor.

56. Bestow rewards without regard to rule, issue orders without regard to previous arrangements; and you will be able to handle a whole army as though you had to do with but a single man.

Once the battle has commenced, a lawyer should finish the case with you. They may never stay with you after the trial is over but again, your oath is to the client and the client alone.

57. Confront your soldiers with the deed itself; never let them know your design. When the outlook is bright, bring it before their eyes; but tell them nothing when the situation is gloomy.

If you let negativity set in, then it is very hard for soldiers or lawyers to keep up their motivation to keep going. If your associate lawyer, for example, thinks they will get a big bonus, but only upon a win, and if they think the hopes of the win has gone, then so will their zeal.

58. Place your army in deadly peril, and it will survive; plunge it into desperate straits, and it will come off in safety.

If you don't keep the team together or on track, the whole case will falter. A bad or flawed team can certainly lose a good case.

59. For it is precisely when a force has fallen into harm's way that is capable of striking a blow for victory.

Desperation breeds miracles. Upsets happen all the time in sport and other areas. You have to keep your team believing they can win, in spite of anything, to keep them properly focused.

60. Success in warfare is gained by carefully accommodating ourselves to the enemy's purpose.

Even if you are Mike Tyson and can throw the best punch in the world, it will only have impact if it lands. The most powerful boxer won't hurt an opponent if their timing and placement of the punch makes it so it doesn't land and make contact. You must know where your opponent is and where they will be in a moment's time to be able to know the timing for your next punch.

61. By persistently hanging on the enemy's flank, we shall succeed in the long run in killing the commander-in-chief.

A direct attack down the middle is rarely successful in war or in law. You have to press the fringes to find a week point that can make the whole centerline crumble.

62. This is called ability to accomplish a thing by sheer cunning.

63. On the day that you take up your command, block the frontier passes, destroy the official tallies, and stop the passage of all emissaries.

Once you have deemed it so that no settlements will be entertained, then you need to make sure your team keeps their mouth shut and doesn't tip off the opponent accidentally either in the hall outside the courtroom or even the hotel bar the night before, or on social media.

64. Be stern in the council-chamber, so that you may control the situation.

There may be pause or hesitation in your team or with the client marking the moment of no return, but you must stand firm if it is the correct decision.

65. If the enemy leaves a door open, you must rush in.

This is always the case. You must be ever vigilant of opportunities when they present themselves. You can't let your commitment to your plan make you miss out on an unexpected option. The decision, at the moment, to deviate or continue when presented with an opening for a new path unique to that case won't be determined by a book or strategic guide. When such a moment arises, you will have to proceed based on your preparation in truly understanding strategy as well the particulars of the unique case itself. Only that preparation and constant work to better yourself will make you able to see the best way forward.

66. Forestall your opponent by seizing what he holds dear, and subtly contrive to time his arrival on the ground.

There are some points that will be made in trial that hurt and are unavoidable. You should always do what you can to have those points come in during better times. If they get buried in the middle of the day rather than the last thing before the jurors recess for the day, it is far less likely to be on their mind that night. It is also always wise to get your counter arguments out sooner so that there is the least amount of time where your opponent presents theories that are unchallenged.

67. Walk in the path defined by rule, and accommodate yourself to the enemy until you can fight a decisive battle.

Patience is a difficult and frustrating skill to master; however, it can be the difference between losing and winning. You have to pick the right time to send discovery material, the right time to expose your previously hidden attack points, to make a switch in demeanor in front of the jury from likable to more aggressive with a witness, etc.

68. At first, then, exhibit the coyness of a maiden, until the enemy gives you an opening; afterwards emulate the rapidity of a running hare, and it will be too late for the enemy to oppose you.

When you decide to do the above and other key items, you should do so with speed to make it harder for the opponent team to respond in kind.

XII. The Attack by Fire

1. Sun Tzu said: There are five ways of attacking with fire. The first is to burn soldiers in their camp; the second is to burn stores; the third is to burn baggage trains; the fourth is to burn arsenals and magazines; the fifth is to hurl dropping fire amongst the enemy.

Such fire in law can be a key piece of evidence or material that you present to the jury through your witness or theirs, generating a spark that can lead to a great argument that engulfs the opponent's critical points their case stands on. Fire in war can go horribly wrong and come back to you and your lines. It must be carefully handled and targeted to the best of your abilities to avoid seeming callous to the jury or taking away too much. For example, if you use 'fire' to discredit the science behind the opponent's expert, then you may also discredit your own expert or the validity of the expertise itself. Fire can be devastating if properly deployed.

2. In order to carry out an attack, we must have means available. The material for raising fire should always be kept in readiness.

Trying to start a conflagration with a tiny spark and no combustible material will not create the intended affect. Fire in law can be powerful attacks and strikes that can have detrimental effect on your case if not handled well. Don't attack an opponent witness with a point that doesn't lead to anything substantial. The hit has to give you something for closing, whether it affects credibility or an element or something other of value.

3. There is a proper season for making attacks with fire, and special days for starting a conflagration.

Timing and environment are key. If you have a powerful attack on a female domestic-assault victim, say during the O.J. Simpson trial, then it may not have the same impact as it would have just the year before. The weather might stifle your sparks or spread the fire to unwanted places or your own part of the field. You must always keep up on current events and the mood of the nation. In the middle of a recession, you don't want your expert witness coming into court dressed in expensive jewelry and other excesses, as it may be a turnoff to the jury before they have even uttered a word, rendering the fire they were to bring ineffective. You don't want a critical witness coming to the stand when the jury is worried about a snowstorm coming in, and they are looking out the window wondering if their kids' school will close early. You can't always control such timing, but if you can, then perhaps switch up the order or delay a witness. You may even try to be the one to propose to the judge in front of the jury that you should get done early so people can get home before a winter storm that is coming.

4. The proper season is when the weather is very dry; the special days are those when the moon is in the constellations of the Sieve, the Wall, the Wing or the Cross-bar; for these four are all days of rising wind.

In opposition to the above: if you are in a recession and can paint the opponent in a civil case as greedy or trying to squeeze out a few bucks by denying an insurance claim, etc. then it can generate a raging fire of hate against your opponent to the point where the jury can't see any opponent's friendly facts beyond the conflagration of hate that you started.

5. In attacking with fire, one should be prepared to meet five possible developments:

6. (1) When fire breaks out inside to enemy's camp, respond at once with an attack from without.

When you have launched incendiary material towards the enemy camp, it can lead the opponent to having to alter their plans to immediately deal with what you have done. If you can raise an issue at trial that forces the opponent off their plan to turn and deal with what you have done, this can seriously alter their flow and also accomplish the goal of getting what you want the jury to be thinking about into their minds, instead of what the opponent had planned for that part of the trial.

7. (2) If there is an outbreak of fire, but the enemy's soldiers remain quiet, bide your time and do not attack.

If you think your launching of inflammatory material has not had its intended effect, then don't continue with your plan, as it is likely not to work. If the opponent is not startled or altering *their* attack, then they at least don't think it is as much of a determent to them as you had hoped. They may, of course, be blinded to its impact by fear, but it is a factor to consider, as you determine what the impact truly will be.

8. (3) When the force of the flames has reached its height, follow it up with an attack, if that is practicable; if not, stay where you are.

If the fire you have thrown has put them off their path or seems to be causing havoc in other ways, then keep the pressure on. The opponent could lose a lot of ground with the jury if they seem disorganized or out of sorts. The more time the opponent spends on trying to stop what you have done and less on what they must build up, the better.

9. (4) If it is possible to make an assault with fire from without, do not wait for it to break out within, but deliver your attack at a favorable moment.

Being able to see what impact your incendiary tool has caused is not always as clear as you would like, as you have to observe it from the outside of their team or through the jury's eyes. Make your best estimate of its impact and act accordingly.

10. (5) When you start a fire, be windward of it. Do not attack from the leeward.

Don't raise a topic that hurts them but also can come back and hurt your arguments that are to occur later. Make sure it is not something that will also discredit your expert, for example. You may want to discredit the work of their expert but not the science of the expertise so that your expert can't be burned with the same material, for example.

11. A wind that rises in the daytime lasts long, but a night breeze soon falls.

A break in between the days of the trial may help your opponent get back on track. Just because they were in great disarray at the end of the day will not mean that they will still be so the next morning. Don't count on them to be the same.

12. In every army, the five developments connected with fire must be known, the movements of the stars calculated, and a watch kept for the proper days.

13. Hence those who use fire as an aid to the attack show intelligence; those who use water as an aid to the attack gain an accession of strength.

If you are to successfully throw an incendiary bomb on their plans, you must know not just the damage it can have but also what recourses the opponent will have to counter. If they have a great way to use water to put out what you have done, then the attack may be seen as a waste of resources or at least not an advantageous time to have use the attack option you can consider.

14. By means of water, an enemy may be intercepted, but not robbed of all his belongings.

You may, if you can try, take steps to affect the opponent's water, i.e. their ability to stop what you plan to do later with an attack. Such variables will differ greatly from case to case and the opponents' abilities. It should not be a new concept for an experienced lawyer to know that you have to ask questions of witnesses or admit exhibits through them that, on their face, mean nothing but when tied together with a later witness or in closing will be a key component of your strategy. You will have to think and plan ahead for such multi-tiered strategies; to not do it is to not fulfill your obligations to your client. If you don't see what your opponent is doing during the trial, it may be too late to have much to counter it with in closings.

15. Unhappy is the fate of one who tries to win his battles and succeed in his attacks without cultivating the spirit of enterprise; for the result is waste of time and general stagnation.

You can't wait for an opportunity to fall into your lap to launch the attack you have planned. You must do all you can ahead of time to build up the material needed and to force the opponent into a position where they will be the most susceptible to it. A boxer does not usually deliver a big punch that knocks out their opponent on its own. It is most often part of an intended combination of punches, jabs, dodges, and repositioning.

16. Hence the saying: The enlightened ruler lays his plans well ahead; the good general cultivates his resources.

No lawyer has ever said: "I regret having prepared so much; I should have done less."

17. Move not unless you see an advantage; use not your troops unless there is something to be gained; fight not unless the position is critical.

It is a key ability of a good trial lawyer to not only build a solid hit or attack but to know when to use it, and if things have changed, to have the modesty and understanding of the current reality to be brave enough to say it won't work and to bide your time or have a strong plan B to move to.

18. No ruler should put troops into the field merely to gratify his own spleen; no general should fight a battle simply out of pique.

Don't be so enraged by the hatred that has built toward your opponent that you let that hatred or spite affect your decisions.

19. If it is to your advantage, make a forward move; if not, stay where you are.

Only attack based on the advantage that you truly believe you can obtain and the reality of the situation regarding the chances that it will work. It may be that you have had a stratagem in your plans for literally months or even years that you can't wait to use, like a kid with a new Christmas morning toy, *but* you must carefully evaluate the lay of the land as it is at the time you are to use it. Keep a clear mind when deciding if a weapon should be used at a particular moment or if at all, based on what has come up at the trial.

20. Anger may in time change to gladness; vexation may be succeeded by content.

You may rejoice for a long time over the wisdom of not having put yourself in a bad position as you made the right call at the critical time. Your frustration in the moment may eventually yield to your team admiring your patience and wisdom, after they see the wisdom of your decision to hold fast.

21. But a kingdom that has once been destroyed can never come again into being; nor can the dead ever be brought back to life.

Always know that if you choose poorly, the client's case may be done for forever. Although you will learn from mistakes and that knowledge may help you in future trials, the client will have only one shot at their case. You certainly don't want to have to be a in a position that is unexplainable with hindsight in a post-conviction relief or appeal hearing.

22. Hence the enlightened ruler is heedful, and the good general full of caution. This is the way to keep a country at peace and an army intact.

Although many decisions must be made in mere moments during the heat of battle, you must know that your bad call can destroy everything. You will not have time to hesitate at the crucial moment, but don't be reckless either. It is easy for us to talk about here, but it is mission-critical to actually know at the crucial time.

XIII. The Use of Spies

1. Sun Tzu said: Raising a host of a hundred thousand men and marching them great distances entails heavy loss on the people and a drain on the resources of the State. The daily expenditure will amount to a thousand ounces of silver. There will be commotion at home and abroad, and men will drop down exhausted on the highways. As many as seven hundred thousand families will be impeded in their labor.

Although not to this extreme, a trial process can be extremely draining to your team and the client/state. Depending on the case type, you have to be aware that the client will be thinking about or be afraid of the outcome of their case, often every day. Your team will spend months and sometimes years on a case, and as you get closer to the end, it will feel like losing the case will be like losing everything. Your team will need to be rallied both regarding their morale and to avoid exhaustion or burnout as well as mental strain.

2. Hostile armies may face each other for years, striving for the victory which is decided in a single day. This being so, to remain in ignorance of the enemy's condition simply because one grudges the outlay of a hundred ounces of silver in honors and emoluments, is the height of inhumanity.

Often you will face lawyers that you know or have worked with. Knowing their personalities, proclivities, and flaws will be critical to your calculations. Knowing about changes in their life, if they have fallen off the wagon, if they are having marital issues, if their child is sick, is all relevant knowledge. You won't know if a lawyer will be off their best, and you certainly can't rely on them having issues, but it is still good to know. Knowing if they are naturally better or worse at certain facets of the case is also mandatory information. For example, depending on the opposition lawyer, I will estimate that I can get more jurors dismissed during jury selection than with other more experienced lawyers. For whatever reason it seems that younger lawyers are more hesitant to object during jury selection than older lawyers. When you are against young opponents, at every stage you are going to be more likely to get close to or step over the line on things if you think your opponent may not see it or not know how to object to what you are doing.

3. One who acts thus is no leader of men, no present help to his sovereign, no master of victory.

"Knowledge is power" is said so often it is like a cliché, but there is still a lot of truth to the statement. Your goal should be to get all the information you can, even if it may only help in a small way. You can't pick the facts or other variables in your case, but you can commit to put forth more effort than the other side.

4. Thus, what enables the wise sovereign and the good general to strike and conquer, and achieve things beyond the reach of ordinary men, is foreknowledge.

To fulfill your obligation to your client, you should leave no ethical stone unturned. Whether it be in the end of the case when you look in the mirror or if you have to answer to the Bar, you need to be able to know or show that you did all you could do.

5. Now this foreknowledge cannot be elicited from spirits; it cannot be obtained inductively from experience, nor by any deductive calculation.

No matter your skill or knowledge of the law or case, information about your opponent will be key. I always tell clients that the truth does not follow us through the courthouse doors, but only what can be shown will be there with us, for better or worse. You are not dealing with a process that always guarantees justice. You must do all you can do, within the rules, to help your client, as the bedrock of our system is adversarial. From the days of Isocrates, the purity of the system only comes from two opposing sides doing all they can for their client. It is the best we have and can only work as best as it can, if the lawyers do everything that they ought to do.

6. Knowledge of the enemy's dispositions can only be obtained from other men.

Lawyers talk; it's our nature. Things can be gleaned from conversations over beers or at events in the community. You should not try to break in to look at files, as there are many other ways and sources to collect information. It can be invaluable to talk to other lawyers about a new opposition to see what they were like in trial or talking to judges who are not on the current case but who have had experience with the opposing lawyer.

7. Hence the use of spies, of whom there are five classes: (1) Local spies; (2) inward spies; (3) converted spies; (4) doomed spies; (5) surviving spies.

8. When these five kinds of spy are all at work, none can discover the secret system. This is called "divine manipulation of the threads." It is the sovereign's most precious faculty.

9. Having local spies means employing the services of the inhabitants of a district.

The local clerks and court reporters, judges, and other lawyers all fall into this category.

10. Having inward spies, making use of officials of the enemy.

This you can't do, but former employees of your opponents are certainly fair game to talk to and get information from.

11. Having converted spies, getting hold of the enemy's spies and using them for our own purposes.

It may be ethical in your jurisdiction for a fellow lawyer to give incorrect information to your opponent, such as that you don't prepare when you do, or your firm is strapped for cash to pay for experts when it is not, or complaining that your team has infighting when it does not. These tactics may not work but they cost you very little to try.

12. Having doomed spies, doing certain things openly for purposes of deception, and allowing our spies to know of them and report them to the enemy.

I have seen lawyers who put on a show that their client is being obstinate and won't take a deal unless they get just a bit more in the offer or have feelers out for information that they really don't care about at all in the hopes it gets back to the opponent. Theoretically you can even have your employees leak information that is not actually true to feed the enemy 'spies' incorrect information that they may act on.

13. Surviving spies, finally, are those who bring back news from the enemy's camp.

If the opponent finds out that you are using a certain person for information, then they should no longer be considered a surviving spy, as you won't trust that what they bring back to you is legitimate.

14. Hence it is that which none in the whole army are more intimate relations to be maintained than with spies. None should be more liberally rewarded. In no other business should greater secrecy be preserved.

Spies should be employed only by you and not members of your team, lest their intent leaks out. By controlling the flow of information yourself, there is less chances of intentional or mistaken leak by your spies or team members using them.

15. Spies cannot be usefully employed without a certain intuitive sagacity.

You can't go on totally blind missions, but you certainly can look for target information based on a case, or the lawyers and judges involved. The missions you choose for them must be between you and them only.

16. They cannot be properly managed without benevolence and straightforwardness.

If you can't trust your spy completely for a task, then you should not be using them at all.

17. Without subtle ingenuity of mind, one cannot make certain of the truth of their reports.

The weight you give to their reports will have to be in large part based on your experience and your knowledge of the parties in play. Without yourself knowing about key characters, you can't properly attribute value to what the source brings you.

18. Be subtle! be subtle! and use your spies for every kind of business.

Never brag about how a clerk gave you information on a past case. Never tell anyone what you have done that may impact your credibility with the court or anyone else. There is no reason not to hold your sources of information close to you, without exception.

19. If a secret piece of news is divulged by a spy before the time is ripe, he must be put to death together with the man to whom the secret was told.

A spy who leaks information via carelessness or malice is the worst kind of spy and one that can't ever be trusted. People working on obtaining information should know more than anyone how valuable key information is. For them to be so careless to leak or divulge secrets is the ultimate indicator that they are not understanding their responsibility. For example, if you talk to a clerk to see how busy the opponent lawyer is for a given window of time, you have to trust that they will not talk about your enquiry to others.

20. Whether the object be to crush an army, to storm a city, or to assassinate an individual, it is always necessary to begin by finding out the names of the attendants, the aides-de-camp, and door-keepers and sentries of the general in command. Our spies must be commissioned to ascertain these.

Knowing who has the information you seek and who you can legally talk to is key. Some judges may know a lot about a lawyer but are not willing to talk about them regardless whether they currently have a case with that lawyer or not. Some judges will deem it acceptable to talk about the other lawyer if there is no current conflict. You must know who will talk and who will not. Some clerks will talk, some will not. Some may go tell others you sought information from them. Some may be closer to your opponent and may want to inform your opponent of what you sought, which can help them predict your plans. People in the world of experts may have information that can help you, such as a state witness who has always given expert findings that the state is correct and never the state's opponent, which may be useful to show that they are pre-disposed and slanted toward the state. You may need a source to obtain that expert's past case history in your jurisdiction and others they have been in that you have not. Learning about an expert saying that there were issues with a similar scientific device used by an officer in other cases may make it easier for you to show that the device doesn't always work in your case. Accident reconstruction experts, breath alcohol experts, and many other types of experts have colleagues that you can reach out to even if you have to pay them for useful information. Some experts see other experts in the same field not as colleagues, but as competing business, and they may love to share information about the expert that you can use against them at trial. There are many ethical ways where you can look for information that can help you from outside the listed witnesses to a case.

21. The enemy's spies who have come to spy on us must be sought out, tempted with bribes, led away and comfortably housed. Thus, they will become converted spies and available for our service.

A better term for such spies to compare them to, as players in war, would be scouts. Having people scout out information for you from legal and ethical sources is far more practical. Of course, you have to be aware that the other side will be seeking out such scouting reports on you as well.

22. It is through the information brought by the converted spy that we are able to acquire and employ local and inward spies.

Often your scouts may simply find other people that can get you the information you need so you can be ready to deal with issues at trial regarding experts or past history of alleged victims, etc. Having a good private investigator to help with your cases is important. You must make sure that they do not overstep the rules or even laws in their efforts to bring you good material.

23. It is owing to his information, again, that we can cause the doomed spy to carry false tidings to the enemy.

If you have a well-off client, you can at times send an investigator to look at something in the hopes that it gets back to your opponent that they did so. Your opponent may take the bait and waste time looking at the red herring you have created. Mentioning something to opposing counsel that you may need to know about can also lead to dead ends and wastes of time for their team.

24. Lastly, it is by his information that the surviving spy can be used on appointed occasions.

Once a spy or counter spy is burned, they are obviously not going to be useful in the future.

25. The end and aim of spying in all its five varieties is knowledge of the enemy; and this knowledge can only be derived, in the first instance, from the converted spy. Hence it is essential that the converted spy be treated with the utmost liberality.

Dealing with anyone who has previously helped your opponent is a most dangerous risk.

26. Of old, the rise of the Yin dynasty was due to I Chih who had served under the Hsia. Likewise, the rise of the Chou dynasty was due to Lu Ya who had served under the Yin.

Former friends can become enemies. Be sure you don't give them too much information about your methods as you never know when they may seek to work for a different lawyer in the future.

27. Hence it is only the enlightened ruler and the wise general who will use the highest intelligence of the army for purposes of spying and thereby they achieve great results. Spies are a most important element in water, because on them depends on an army's ability to move.

Useful information is key. Knowing it is useful or accurate will depend on you and knowing the quality and intelligence from your scout. You may employ scouts or staff on a mission simply to try to verify information you have received from another source. Spy or scout usage can come with risks, but to ignore them altogether can be deadly for your client. To presume your opponent is not using them is also a potentially fatal mistake.

About the Author

Daniel J. Rothman has been practicing criminal law since 2002, having taken more than thirty cases before a jury. He is a former prosecutor with seven years' experience and has been a criminal defense attorney since 2009. During his time as a prosecutor, Mr. Rothman was an instructor for the Prosecutors Training Council's Annual Officer's training school and a presenter for the Central Iowa Traffic Safety Task Force's annual training regarding OWI/DUI law. Mr. Rothman was invited to teach other attorneys how to handle OWI/DUI cases in 2011 by the Law Review CLE Group. He prosecuted many types of major felony cases including burglary, sex assault, narcotic offenses, and white-collar crimes. He is also a graduate of the Trial Advocacy program at the National District Attorney's Association's National Advocacy Center at the University of South Carolina.

As a defense attorney, Mr. Rothman has represented clients in a wide variety of cases from petty crimes to murder. He has also taken his clients' arguments to the Iowa Supreme Court where he obtained victories for his clients on such issues as illegal searches for narcotics and violations of clients' rights to attorney consultation.

He received both his law degree and his Bachelor of Arts in Rhetoric and History, from Drake University.